NIKI
LAUDA

By ALAN HENRY

HAZLETON PUBLISHING

PUBLISHER
Richard Poulter

EXECUTIVE PUBLISHER
Elizabeth Le Breton

ART EDITOR
Steve Small

EXECUTIVE PRODUCTION MANAGER
George Greenfield

PRODUCTION CONTROLLER
Peter Lovering

PRODUCTION ASSISTANT
Deirdre Fenney

STATISTICS
John Taylor

Colour photography by:

Front and back cover   –   Paul-Henri Cahier
Pages 65-76   –   David Phipps
Pages 77-78   –   Paul-Henri Cahier
Pages 79-80   –   David Phipps

Black and white photographs contributed by:
Jeff Bloxham, Diana Burnett, Bernard Cahier, International
Press Agency, LAT, David Phipps, Steve Small, Nigel Snowdon
and Keith Sutton.

This first edition published in 1989 by
Hazleton Publishing, 3 Richmond Hill, Richmond,
Surrey TW10 6RE.

ISBN: 0-905138-68-6

Printed in England by BAS Printers Ltd, Over Wallop,
Hampshire.

Typesetting by First Impression Graphics Ltd, Richmond,
Surrey.

DISTRIBUTOR

UK & OTHER MARKETS
Osprey Publishing Limited, 59 Grosvenor Street,
London W1X 9DA

*Youthful innocence, summer of 1971, just prior to his first
try in an F1 car. The toothy grin endures to this day...*

PROLOGUE

This book not only sets out to provide an account of a triple World Champion's career but also, I hope, tells the reader something about Niki Lauda's personality. If you want to read the man's own inner thoughts on various aspects of his life and career, he has penned at least three first-person accounts which are available in the English language. But within these pages I've attempted to project an idea of what Lauda is like, his essential honesty and directness, his humour and his tenacity. So this is an informal over-view of Niki's career, a portrait of the man rather than a detailed biography.

In many ways, like Jackie Stewart, Mario Andretti, Gilles Villeneuve and Alain Prost, Niki Lauda was always a journalist's dream. While others hummed and haahed, wondering whether it was prudent or diplomatic to say this or that, Lauda would speak his mind and rely on the interviewer to quote him correctly. That, in itself, was another pretty straightforward task because he always got right to the point. His directness could sometimes be startling, with a dry wit which often went right over some people's heads. In fact, he has a very English sense of humour which I'm certain was forged during his formative years in F2 in 1971-72.

He was a fine Grand Prix driver, of that there is no shadow of a doubt. If I believe, more than some, that he was a pivotal force within his own era, I hope I haven't reached that conclusion simply because I like him so much. He was too much of a pragmatist to be swept away on the extrovert, romantic flood tide that made the likes of Villeneuve and Peterson, for example, such archetypal motor racing heroes. Yet he had a wide enough understanding of the nature of motor racing as a sport to hold these charismatic personalities in high regard. In his view, they simply approached the same task from subtly different angles.

In the ultimate analysis, Niki Lauda's name will go down in motor racing folklore for the heroism and singlemindedness he applied to the 1976 season. When, after suffering the awful consequences of that fiery accident in the German Grand Prix, he hauled himself back into the cockpit of his Ferrari in an attempt to defend his World Championship, he crossed that ill-defined frontier which delineates the territory of a sporting star from that of an international celebrity.

He was unsuccessful in his quest to retain the title, but it was a glorious failure which, paradoxically, considerably enhanced his reputation. But there were other races and achievements which gave him much more satisfaction than his 1976 performances and it irked him mildly that so many people held up that championship battle as the high spot of his racing career. There were other races at other times which gave him equal, if not greater, fulfilment.

Although he irritated the traditionalists with the way in which he calculated the odds in ruthlessly dispassionate fashion, then drove accordingly, he was a great – rather than a good – racing driver. In my mind there could be no greater endorsement of that fact than the reception the Brands Hatch crowd accorded him when he won both the 1982 and '84 British Grands Prix.

For some reason, like Ronnie Peterson before him, Lauda struck a certain chord with the knowledgeable British race fans. As he cruised those two slowing-down laps there were no histrionics, no fists punching the air, no weeping or banging the side of his helmet. Just a forefinger raised from the cockpit in polite and appreciative thanks for their support. It was a small detail, delightfully understated.

On both occasions, the crowd simply went wild with delight...

Max Mosley and Robin Herd both reached the conclusion that there were few other drivers of their era temperamentally better suited to win a World Championship title. Unfortunately, this outstandingly prescient observation, first made to me by Herd in 1972, was blighted by their rider – 'but the only thing I question is whether he has enough speed to get to the top.'

Self-confidence was never a quality that seemed to be lacking in Niki Lauda's make-up, although he always kept the pressure cooker of ambition simmering just below boiling point. It was as if he were involved in a complex and tactical game of chess. The buck-toothed lad from Vienna – who, by his own admission, looked a bit of a drip when his parents dressed him up in traditional Austrian garb as a schoolboy – came from an extremely well-off family with interests in the financial world. His grandfather once told him, early in his racing career, that he was not interested in seeing Niki's name on the sports pages of the newspapers. But if he made it onto the financial pages, that was another matter altogether...

Born in the Austrian capital on 22 February 1949, the scion of a wealthy family who owned several paper processing plants, Niki had a conventional and formal upbringing as befitted the eldest son of an Austrian of some substance. His father quickly recognised his son's enthusiasm for mechanical matters and

Wrestling with the F3 McNamara at Brands Hatch, 1970. Niki's efforts with the German-built car went almost totally unnoticed.

Taking it carefully with his Porsche 908 during the Yellow Pages Trophy race at Thruxton, late summer 1970. Niki was so conscious of the amount of money invested in this machine that he never so much as spun it, let alone put it off the circuit anywhere!

Left: *Getting a lift into the pits at Rouen on the back of Ronnie Peterson's March 712M, 1971. The way he kept pace with Ronnie during the first heat of this F2 international was the first sign of Niki's long-term potential.*

Middle: *Strapped into his works 'renta March' prior to his Grand Prix debut at the Österreichring, 1971. He retired the 711 with handling problems.*

Right: *Niki and Ronnie Peterson got on like a house on fire. They shared a distinctly Anglicised sense of humour, with a ready wit and a well-developed sense of fun, as well as being extremely close friends.*

attempted, with little success, to steer the boy along a more academic path.

The same year as Niki was born, the Lauda family acquired a Volkswagen which was to play an important role in nurturing his embryonic enthusiasm for cars and motoring. After serving its time as the family hack, it was passed down to the children who used it to crash around the grounds of their home. Thus Niki was able to make a considerable nuisance of himself while at the same time learning about the fundamentals of car control.

Niki's grandparents lived close to one of the family factories, about 70 miles from Vienna, and this was where he recalls many happy summer holidays. Hours were spent getting filthy dirty in the factory workshops where he encountered an understandable degree of deference from the workforce, and a reluctance to allow him to become too involved.

'It was pretty difficult to persuade the fitters to let me change the oil, for example,' he said, many years later, 'because I was the boss's son and they were afraid to let me get really dirty. Eventually they used to loosen the sump plugs right off until they were nearly out, and I was allowed to unscrew them for the final turn. I regarded that as a great achievement!'

From mastering this technique, Niki soon went on to become something of a dab hand at handling a forklift truck, and he celebrated his fifteenth birthday by actually starting to drive the firm's lorries on short trips from one factory to another. This enterprise was to land him in considerable trouble.

'All the local police knew who I was, and were always extremely courteous, waving me through when I appeared at the wheel of this truck,' he recounted. 'I was never stopped by any of them. The trouble was, of course, that on my eighteenth birthday, I had to go along to the same police station to ask for the application form for a driving licence...' Niki recalls that the officer on duty almost choked with indignation, but the whole matter was eventually smoothed over.

Niki's academic achievements by this stage were distinctly average. He had almost no interest in his studies, much like the great Jochen Rindt whose mantle as Austria's top Grand Prix driver he would later assume. In 1966 he visited the German Grand Prix at the Nürburgring – won by Jack Brabham's Brabham-Repco after a wet-weather tussle with John Surtees's Cooper-Maserati – and from that moment realised he simply had to go racing. In fact, his entire efforts thereafter were exclusively aimed at securing himself some

*Heading for seventh place in the 1972 South African
Grand Prix at Kyalami with the works March 721. He
finished feet behind Graham Hill's Brabham BT33 after
what Niki later described as 'one of the best driving
lessons I've ever had'.*

sort of racing car.

Although only 17, his road car at the time was a Mini Cooper S and he admits to being sorely tempted when he noticed that a full race version had been put up for sale by a local ace called Fritz Baumgarten. Niki made up his mind that he was going to have the car, come what may, but there was no way in the world he could persuade his family to help with any financial support. Doubly determined he telephoned Baumgarten, offering the sort of deal that showed considerable commercial acumen for one of such tender years.

'I told him I was interested and wanted to examine the car in more detail, and invited him to bring it round to my house,' Niki recalled. 'When he arrived, I offered him a deal whereby I would exchange my road car for his racer and pay him the difference between the value of the two cars when I sold the racer.' Niki recalls that Baumgarten glanced round the imposing Lauda residence and did the deal, presumably figuring that if Niki didn't pay, there was somebody else sufficiently wealthy within the family who would...

Lauda's bare-faced nerve was remarkable. He then went to his father and explained he had a friend who had a racing Mini Cooper 'and could he keep it in our garage as he hasn't got anywhere under cover to put it?' His father agreed. Niki's first competitive outing was at the Mühllacken hill climb. He set off with Baumgarten in a BMW 2800, towing the Mini Cooper. His father thought he was just going along to help.

Despite taking it easy to conserve the engine, Lauda finished second in class. It was all over the sports pages of the Vienna newspapers the next morning, a fact that made Niki's efforts to bluff his father into believing he hadn't been racing a trifle difficult. Lauda senior was absolutely livid and expressly forbade any further competition outings. Using a certain amount of subterfuge, Niki spirited the Mini Cooper off to the next hill climb fixture at Dobratsch. This time he won his class.

'My father went mad again,' he recalls; it was almost the end of their relationship. Niki wasted very little time in moving away from Vienna to Salzburg and settling down with his girlfriend Mariella Reininghaus, a member of the famous Austrian brewing dynasty. A delightful, slender, incredibly placid girl with considerable presence, she did a lot to underpin Niki's morale in those early days. They were inseparable companions for seven years.

Almost unbelievably, Niki managed to repeat his earlier deal with Baumgarten when it came to purchasing a Porsche 911S off fellow-Austrian Peter Peter. 'Double Pete', as he was known by many, agreed that he should pay the balance of the purchase price when he sold the car. It would later become clear that such apparently outrageous business propositions were absolutely characteristic of the man.

If Niki worried about the financial hot water he got himself into throughout those early years, he never betrayed a trace of that concern. He'd charted his chosen path, and if sheer talent wasn't going to get him there, he would raise sponsorship, loans or whatever.

His 911S programme almost became seriously derailed at the Koralpe hill climb later in 1968: 'I arrived driving my Porsche on the road, whereas all the opposition brought theirs along in trailers. Of course, I forgot that, after I'd fitted the racing exhaust, the thing was going to shoot along a little bit quicker. The inevitable happened: I bounced off a wall and shot off down the mountain, into a ditch.'

Everybody thought the whole episode extremely amusing, feeling that this upstart had received his long-overdue come-uppance. They laughed on the other side of their faces, though, when the committed Lauda manhandled his Porsche from the ditch and breezed through to win the Group 2 class – beating all the more powerful Group 5 machinery in the process.

For 1969, he was invited to have a try in one of the works Austro Kaimann Formula Vee cars. At Hockenheim, a track on which Formula Vee racing seemed like premeditated lunacy, Niki did the lion's share of leading before spinning off near the finish. Foolishly, he began to feel over-confident.

'The next day I rushed down to the airfield race at Aspern, honestly believing I must be the greatest racing driver of all time.

'The organisers laid on a special late morning practice session for me on the Sunday morning, but during the race I somehow managed to try tackling a corner on which two other cars had already spun and blocked the track...' The Kaimann cartwheeled to destruction, its remains scattered the length and breadth of the airfield's main runway. Niki walked away unscathed, but very thoughtful. On a more successful note, he set the first sub 10-minute Formula Vee lap at the Nürburgring, although his arch-rival, compatriot Helmut Marko, went on to win the race.

The following year he was offered an F3 drive with Francis McNamara's

*Niki's wet-weather victory at Oulton Park on Good
Friday, 1972 with the STP March 722 offered an
interesting pointer to his future form.*

Later in the year, his March now sporting a front radiator,
Niki sped to second place behind Ronnie Peterson at the
same circuit, recording fastest lap in the process (bottom).
However, before the race he had seemed anything but
hopeful about the outcome (below).

Left: *Team-mates can be friends: Niki with Ronnie Peterson.*

Below left: *Niki practising a works 721 at Vallelunga prior to the non-title F1 race held at the Rome circuit in June 1972. Soon after this shot was taken, he wrecked the 721 and consequently failed to make the start.*

team, operating out of a base at Lenngries, between Munich and Salzburg. However, finance proved wholly inadequate and Niki got involved in a series of hair-raising accidents as he attempted to keep up. Mid-way through the year he changed horses again, borrowing heavily to acquire a Porsche 908 sports racer. 'I was so nervous about damaging the thing that I never once so much as spun it, never mind going off the track,' he says.

Of course, 1970 was a year peppered with motor racing tragedy, with Austrian fans mourning the loss of the great Jochen Rindt, killed when his Lotus 72 crashed during practice for the Italian Grand Prix at Monza. Niki was never one for hero worship. He had a great deal of admiration for Jochen, but it would be absurd to attribute to him a mission to follow in Rindt's footsteps. None the less, having lost its national hero, Austria became extremely interested in the progress of its new motor racing generation over the next few years, which stood to benefit not only Niki, but also his compatriots Helmut Marko and Dieter Quester.

There were plans mooted for a national Austrian F2 team, involving both Lauda and Marko, but that was a rather unrealistic dream. Instead, Niki went out and raised £8500 worth of sponsorship from a bank – the Erste Osterreichische Sparkasse – and beat a path to March Engineering's door at Bicester to secure a seat in the ambitious 'renta drive' team which was being put together alongside Ronnie Peterson's works effort.

Under the good-natured yet eagle-eyed management of Peter Briggs, this caravan of Marches included Peterson's factory entry, the 'renta cars' of Lauda and Mike Beuttler, plus occasional entries for the Jean-Pierres, Jaussaud and Jarier, under the Shell/Arnold banner. Wearing a sheepskin coat several sizes too big for him, Niki appeared in the paddock at Mallory Park for the first non-title race of the season. It was a bitterly cold day and he looked like a sheepish little lost kid.

I was lucky enough to grow up with Lauda's generation, moving into F1 as a journalist only a year after he did, and I've had the privilege of watching many fine Grand Prix races, a significant number of which have seen Niki playing a pivotal role. But there's no doubt that everybody involved will recall the 1971 European F2 season as a particularly special year, offering a degree of camaraderie that has probably never been experienced subsequently.

The racing was also excellent, in part due to the fact that it was the last season of the 1.6-litre F2 regulations – in which the Cosworth FVA four-cylinder had proved every bit as remarkable a customer engine as the DFV in F1 – but also because a new wave of driving talent was beginning to surge through, heading for the Grand Prix arena.

In those early years Niki was rather shy, a fact that may seem strange to those who became acquainted with him later in his F1 career. He had yet to acquire that patina of relaxed, clipped confidence which was to become the hallmark of his World Championship years. In company with Mariella, he drove round Europe in a blue Porsche 911S, renting a mews flat near London's Victoria Station from Max Mosley when he was staying in England. His grasp of English was initially faltering, but the speed at which he became fluent during 1971 provided another small index of his determination. In that respect he comfortably outstripped dear old Ronnie Peterson who, by comparison, remained on the nursery slopes of the English language right through to the end of his life.

For those with long memories, 1971 was the time when the zany, off-beat humour of John Cleese and his cohorts brought *Monty Python's Flying Circus* to the British television screen. At the mere mention of 'Albatross' and 'Gannet on a stick', everybody in the March F2 team simply fell about in fits of mirth. Surrounded by what they clearly must have regarded as a lorryload of lunatics, Niki and Ronnie found themselves propelled into this peculiar world of specialised English humour. While they joined in with great willingness, I always had the impression that they were waiting for the men in white coats to usher everybody away. Niki had only the most superficial grasp of what in heaven's name we were all on about, but he smiled indulgently and was always enormous fun to be with. Mariella clearly thought we were all barking mad.

From a racing standpoint, the year was only partly successful. Truth be told, you had to be looking closely to see signs of Niki's burgeoning talent, though if you scratched away it was certainly there. Engine unreliability blighted his efforts, but he ran superbly well at the Rouen-les-Essarts road circuit, challenging Ronnie for the lead of his F2 heat and even poking his March 712M into the lead for a lap or so, much to the consternation of March director Alan Rees who almost fell out of his pit as he frantically signalled the Austrian to get back into second place again.

'With age on his side, and if he doesn't allow himself to be disheartened by retirements, bad luck or progress too quickly, then Niki Lauda's ability may

perhaps earn him a regular place in F1 in a couple of season's time.' I gave that rather cautious nod of approval to Niki's career prospects in *Motoring News* in the summer of 1971, at a time when I was feeling my way behind a typewriter rather more than he was in the March. But several of us, including Pete Briggs, sensed that he was going to be good – and not necessarily altogether based on his performances in the cockpit. What was becoming clear by the end of that year was his air of unflappable self-confidence. He may have been the youngest kid on the block, but he was certainly the coolest customer.

In September 1971 I well remember lying sick in a hotel room at Albi when there was a knock on the door. It was the youthful Lauda with a rather serious question.

'I've just signed an F1 contract with March for 1972,' he said briskly, 'and I've got to transfer £32,000 to their bank account in Bicester by the end of next week. But my sponsors have pulled out. What should I do?' What had happened was that he'd done a deal with a Vienna bank, but his grandfather – whom he never referred to as anything but 'Old Lauda' – intervened on the financial grapevine and got the agreement withdrawn. Niki had gone ahead on the basis that the sponsorship was, in effect, in the bank, signing the deal with Max. The plan was that he should drive as Ronnie's number two in the STP-backed works team, taking in a limited programme of F2 events for the factory as well.

Mosley, of course, was leaning on him quite heavily, reminding him that there was a queue of drivers stretching down from the March factory into the centre of Bicester, all waiting for Niki to drop out so that they could purchase the drive alongside Peterson. There wasn't, of course, but this strategy was a great way to keep up the pressure.

Eventually Niki got the money together by mortgaging his life against a bank loan. It was a complex arrangement which involved another Austrian bank, the Raiffeisenkasse, advancing him the money, securing it in the event of an unfortunate accident by means of a life insurance policy. Whatever happened, of course, Niki would have to repay the money. In 1971, £32,000 was an absolutely massive sum. Many people believed that Lauda had taken leave of his senses.

Niki had enjoyed – if that's the word – a preliminary run in a Grand Prix car at the Österreichring in 1971, renting a spare works March 711 for his home Grand Prix. Predictably it had failed to last the distance, but he had rightly convinced himself that March were the logical people with whom to stay. He thought seriously about doing a deal with John Surtees, perhaps for Formula 5000 if he couldn't raise an F1 budget, and visited Big John's Edenbridge base during August 1971 for discussions. But nothing came of it and he went on to do the March deal.

At the start of the 1972 season March relied on the 721, an uprated version of the previous year's machine which Ronnie Peterson had used to finish second in the World Championship, behind Jackie Stewart. However, March designer Robin Herd had grandiose plans for an ambitious new car, a machine which would redefine F1 car performance. It was the March 721X which, with its inboard Alfa Romeo-based gearbox, would almost finish the careers of everybody who had anything to do with it. Its utter and complete failure seriously damaged Herd's reputation as an F1 engineer, reduced Peterson to a state of utter bewilderment and left Lauda wondering whether perhaps he couldn't drive racing cars after all, and that 1971 had been a rather pleasant dream.

Even when March rushed the hastily conceived 721G – based round their F2 chassis – into service mid-season, it could not salvage the team's fortunes. It was an improvement, admittedly, but in the summer of 1972 Mosley and Herd were desperately concentrating their efforts on trying to keep Peterson from the clutches of Colin Chapman. What happened to Niki was not really a priority. His was a purely business arrangement. They'd taken his money and provided him with a racing car. The obligation went no further than that.

When Niki told Robin that the 721X was 'no bloody good' after a few practice laps for the Spanish Grand Prix at Járama, Herd replied: 'When you have as much experience as Ronnie then you, too, will be able to get the best from this car.' Ronnie, of course, was floundering around, as lost as anybody else with the 721X. About six months later, Robin Herd told me, 'I wish we'd taken more notice of him earlier in the year. We owe him a terrific moral obligation…' They should have taken more notice of his F2 performances in the works March 722, as well, notably his superb wet-weather win at Oulton Park in the first round of the John Player British national championship.

That was as maybe, of course, but March effectively put Niki out on the street. Ten years later, the way in which they did it still irked Lauda.

'The one thing that kept me going through 1972 was the fact that, when we went testing, I was virtually as quick as Ronnie,' he recalled with pleasure. 'But when they kicked me out at the end of the season, well, that was my lowest moment….Christ, I mean, I had a loan to repay. Yes, that's right, Mr Mosley waited until November before telling me, I thought that was very helpful of him. And that was after he'd been telling me "yes, you get the drive for next year, no problems. We have a car for you and it's all going to be fine, blah, blah, blah…" and then, suddenly, I have nothing.'

Niki's escape route came in the form of a drive for the Marlboro BRM team, achieved by pulling something of a flanker on Jean Stanley's husband who was running the team at the time. The opportunistic Lauda called up Louis Stanley and indicated that he might well have a sponsor in the pipeline. Stanley took the bait and the two men got together. Niki pledged a further £80,000 worth of sponsorship, publicly hoping that the Raiffeisenkasse would continue extending its support, but privately nursing grave doubts. In the event, he came up with a clever schedule of sponsorship payments, the basis of which was that he would pay 'in arrears', hoping that his earnings from F1 and his BMW Alpina touring car contracts would be sufficient to make the first payment. Inwardly, he knew he would have to produce some spectacular form in the first few races to employ as a bargaining counter to renegotiate the terms of his contract mid-season.

At the end of 1973, just prior to making the break to Ferrari, Niki said of BRM: 'No, I didn't pay for that drive. I spoke to Marlboro about it and they helped me, but they didn't pay.'

At Monaco, of course, Niki qualified the BRM P160 in sixth place, then moved up to third in the race, holding station behind Stewart's Tyrrell and Fittipaldi's Lotus for many laps before the gearbox broke. 'To start with, I was told I could only do the first three Grands Prix because Vern Schuppan was then due to take over alongside Jean-Pierre Beltoise and Clay Regazzoni,' he grins, 'but then in South Africa I was the quickest BRM in one of the practice sessions and, after they took my car away to give to Clay, I was still fastest in the P160 he discarded.

'It was at that point that Stanley decided I could run for the rest of the season, particularly in view of the fact that Clay had just had that serious accident at Kyalami. I kept the drive, luckily I suppose, because I was quicker than Schuppan. Looking back on it, BRM was very much a last ditch attempt to salvage something of a racing career, so I was really lucky, I suppose.'

At the wheel of the BRM P160 during the South African GP at Kyalami where he first made the point that he was quicker than fellow team-drivers Jean-Pierre Beltoise and Clay Regazzoni.

After Monaco, Lauda came clean with Stanley and confessed that he hadn't got the necessary sponsorship to do the year. The BRM boss, delighted by his new protégé's performance in this prestigious event, suggested that the sponsorship instalment arrangement be forgotten. Niki would be paid as a regular driver, provided he signed a contract for 1974 and '75. Lauda, without any choice, reached for the pen.

At Monaco, however, he had also attracted the attention of Enzo Ferrari. Curious to know more about this young Austrian who had kept ahead of Ickx's Ferrari 312B3 – a truly rotten F1 car, it has to be said – the Commendatore instructed his men in the field to keep an eye on Lauda's progress. Although Niki would only score one helping of championship points for BRM during the course of the year (fifth at Zolder in the Belgian Grand Prix) he sustained his position as the most consistently impressive of the team's drivers.

Tim Parnell was BRM team-manager at the time and has vivid recollections of Lauda's singlemindedness. 'He was 100 per cent determined, to the same sort of level as Graham Hill had been. There was no doubt at all in his own mind that he would make the grade. As a driver he was really terrific and he had a level of testing ability which I'd previously only ever encountered with Mike Spence. He could detect shortcomings in the chassis performance, identify what needed to be changed and the car would respond immediately when we made that change. He was a really good chap to work with, who knew what he wanted and always gave the impression that he was in complete control. He applied the knowledge gained with BRM to great effect.'

In the summer of 1973 Niki was contacted by Luca Montezemolo, a young member of the Agnelli dynasty who had been installed at Maranello as a liaison man between Ferrari and Fiat. Shrewd, intelligent and ambitious, Luca would act as a buffer between the Ferrari racing department and the political 'underground' which inevitably attempted to bend the Old Man's ear when the cars were away from base competing in the races.

Niki found himself involved in some pretty clever legal juggling to unload his continuing obligation to BRM. 'It was a tricky operation,' he conceded, 'but I had another slice of luck because BRM was in a weak financial position. I eventually got off the hook by proving that Mr Stanley said he would be paying me some money which I never actually saw. That enabled me to get out of the contract.'

But he admitted the BRM P160 hadn't been a bad car: 'Really, the chassis was very competitive and I found I could keep up with the opposition through all the corners with no problem, particularly later in the year when Firestone came up with some very much better tyres than we'd been using earlier in the season. But the V12 engine simply hadn't got the necessary power. It was ludicrous. We were just left standing on the straights when it came to acceleration and top speed.' But the way in which he surged into second place behind Stewart's Tyrrell at the restart of the British Grand Prix, and simply left the opposition in his spray during the early laps at Mosport Park, put his true potential on very public view.

Moving to Ferrari catapulted Niki Lauda into a new motor racing dimension. For all their sponsorship gloss, BRM had been treading the sunset path for a couple of seasons by the time Niki arrived on the scene. It was a case of cobbled-up gearboxes and patched-up cylinder blocks hidden beneath a flashy paint job. The tempo of F1 was speeding up dramatically in the early 1970s and BRM's management, all tradition and protocol, was being left behind. Niki jumped ship at the last possible moment to save what was left of his career.

For 1974, Ferrari based its efforts round a heavily revamped version of the 312B3 as raced by Arturo Merzario in the last few races of the '73 season. Designer Mauro Forghieri had moved the cockpit and fuel cells some five inches further forward and exhaustive development work had brought the flat-12 3-litre engine to within striking distance of 500 bhp. That, Forghieri reasoned, should be sufficient to see off anybody with a Cosworth DFV. And, as things turned out, it was.

Niki was paired with Clay Regazzoni, the Swiss having resumed his position on the Maranello driving strength after a year's abortive sabbatical with BRM. The two men, widely differing in temperament, got along famously well, Clay's straightforward and uncomplicated approach to life and living acting as a useful counterpoint to Niki's on-track intensity. By this stage, Niki's pronounced front teeth had earned him the nickname of 'Super Mouse'. Over the years that followed, this soubriquet would be modified to 'Super Rat', 'King Rat' – and finally he would be referred to simply as 'The Rat'. Not the most flattering of handles, perhaps, but Niki enjoyed it...

They finished second and third in the opening race at Buenos Aires, Niki chasing Denny Hulme's winning Marlboro McLaren across the line. It was a

*Lauda berates the author, doubtless over something he had
written, during practice for the 1974 British GP.
Montezemolo (left) tries to keep awake.*

Top: Niki and his long-time girlfriend Mariella
Reininghaus share an umbrella with Ferrari's Luca
Montezemolo.

Above: Niki's Ferrari B3 eases into Kyalami's
Crowthorne corner just ahead of Carlos Reutemann's
Brabham BT44, while Regazzoni tries to squeeze his
B3 past the Brabham on an even tighter line. Jody
Scheckter's Tyrrell, Arturo Merzario's Williams and
Emerson Fittipaldi's McLaren M23 are ranged out
across the track in the next rank.

good start but, as the season developed, it became clear that McLaren's new recruit, Emerson Fittipaldi, was adopting a tactical approach in his efforts to win a second World Championship. Although Hulme had won that first race of the year, Fittipaldi was by far the most consistent front runner. And the Brazilian would profit by Ferrari's two drivers splitting the laurels between them.

Lauda matured as a driver in leaps and bounds throughout 1974, aided enormously by Ferrari's resources. He quickly identified that intensive testing was the key to consistent race performances and, with the Ferrari test track situated right next to the factory, he was in a strong position to put as many miles as he wanted under his belt.

He drove magnificently to win the rain-spoiled Spanish Grand Prix at Járama and the Dutch Grand Prix at Zandvoort, the latter a commanding performance from the front of the field. But his lack of experience cost him dear at several other events. He crashed on the opening lap at the Nürburgring, handing Regazzoni victory on a plate, and also slid off the road at Mosport Park when he apparently had the Canadian Grand Prix all buttoned up. A puncture robbed him of the lead in the British Grand Prix at Brands Hatch – and the humiliating incompetence of the RAC resulted in him finding the pit exit lane blocked by a crowd of hangers-on when he attempted to rejoin the fray. That was one of the few times he was seen, publicly, close to tears.

The way in which Montezemolo provided a sympathetic, and accurate, line of communication between the racing team and Mr Ferrari was particularly appreciated by Lauda. 'He got everybody going with a tremendous sense of purpose,' says Niki firmly, 'and he kept the Old Man informed of what was going on with absolute objectivity. Of course, those lines of communication hadn't always been so objective in the past!'

Niki learned a great deal from his driving errors in 1974, emerging at the start of the following year an even more polished, relaxed and assured performer. This coincided with the arrival of Mauro Forghieri's superb 312T (for *trasversale*), the latest variation on the flat-12 engined theme but with a transverse gearbox situated ahead of the rear axle-line in an attempt to produce the lowest polar moment of inertia. Forghieri had rather more success, in this respect, than Robin Herd.

Niki freely admits that he wasn't convinced about the 312T when Forghieri

first outlined his plans, but when he sampled the new car at Fiorano he suddenly appreciated what an enormous quantum leap forward it represented. The 'B3' had always been prone to a slight touch of understeer. No matter how its chassis was adjusted, it seemed impossible to rid the machine of this abiding quality. The 312T proved as near neutral as could be imagined. Nervous to drive close to the limit of adhesion, admittedly, but that limit seemed significantly higher than most of the opposition's.

The new cars were not ready until the third round of the World Championship at Kyalami where Niki trailed home a disappointing fifth, subsequently relieved when he was told that the metering unit drive belt had stripped some teeth and was slipping badly. When the engine was put back on the Maranello test bed, it was revealed to be producing a mere 440 bhp...

Thankfully, this was one of the few mechanical problems experienced with the 312T during the course of that glorious summer. Lauda set the tone of the season by winning the non-title International Trophy by less than a length from Emerson Fittipaldi's McLaren M23, then suffered another slight hiccup when Mario Andretti's Parnelli punted him into team-mate Clay Regazzoni on the run down to the first corner in the Spanish Grand Prix. Niki had started from pole position on Barcelona's fabulous Montjuich Park road circuit, but was at least spared any involvement in the tragic accident later in the day, when Rolf Stommelen's Hill GH1 vaulted the barrier into a restricted area, killing four onlookers.

Niki and the 312T were up and running from Monaco onwards, winning commandingly through the tortuous streets. He repeated the success at Zolder, venue for the Belgian Grand Prix, then silenced those critics who said the Ferrari's power surplus was the only significant factor by tenaciously hauling in Carlos Reutemann's Brabham BT44B to win the Swedish GP at Anderstorp.

His fourth victory at Paul Ricard flowed freely, but he experienced a few hiccups, notably when he was defeated by James Hunt's Hesketh 308 in the Dutch GP at Zandvoort, giving him a foretaste of the championship battle to follow in 1976. The British GP at Silverstone turned out to be a chaotic fiasco for Ferrari, Niki winding up eighth in an event brought to a premature halt by a thunderstorm. A puncture dropped him to third at the Nürburgring and he trailed

Top: *First victory at Monaco: stooping to kiss Princess Grace's hand in suitably gallant fashion.*

Above: *Heading for a hard-fought victory in the 1975 Swedish GP with the Ferrari 312 T.*

Drivers' briefing for the 1975 British GP. Left to right: *the late Carlos Pace, Emerson Fittipaldi, Jody Scheckter, an obviously weary Clay Regazzoni, Lella Lombardi, Vittorio Brambilla, Niki and Carlos Reutemann.*

home sixth in torrential rain after getting caught out by wrong chassis settings
in front of his home crowd at the Österreichring.

At Monza, with the World Championship there for the asking, he played safe
and clinched the title with a third place (Regazzoni won) and then wound up
the year by beating Fittipaldi in the US GP at Watkins Glen, not without a little
intervention by Regazzoni who was eventually blackflagged out of the race for
balking the McLaren driver. This provoked an unpleasant scene in the pits
when Montezemolo almost came to blows with SCCA director, Burdette
Martin, an unfortunate note on which to end an otherwise splendid year.

Congratulations! Being interviewed by respected commentator Chris Economaki at Watkins Glen (top left) and, in the rather more formal surroundings of the FIA's Paris headquarters (right), by Prince Metternich (left) and the CSI's Pierre Ugeux.

Main picture: Chased by Emerson Fittipaldi's McLaren, Niki leads the opening lap of the 1975 United States GP at Watkins Glen. This was to be his fifth race victory of the season.

Above: *More of the same. Niki kicked off 1976 on a similarly victorious note, winning the Brazilian GP at Interlagos. Here he is sharing the rostrum with Patrick Depailler and Tom Pryce, respectively second and third.*

*Mr and Mrs Lauda. Niki and Marlene at the 1976
Swedish Grand Prix, shortly after their whirlwind
courtship and marriage.*

The next two seasons were to see Niki Lauda display the true quality of his determination and commitment. For 1976 his most formidable opposition would come from his good friend James Hunt, now recruited into the Marlboro McLaren fold since Hesketh had effectively closed its doors as a front-line team; Fittipaldi had made a disastrous career move, joining the team established by his elder brother Wilson.

Moreover, there were changes afoot at Ferrari. Montezemolo moved on to pursue his career within the Fiat empire and his place was taken by the gregarious Daniele Audetto, former Lancia competitions boss. Niki found him a touch too flash for his own personal taste and lost no time in setting out the ground rules governing their relationship. On race morning at Interlagos, prior to the start of the Brazilian GP, for instance, Audetto was fussing around Lauda, advising him that it was time to put on his helmet and be strapped into the cockpit. Niki flashed him a glance. 'I'll let you know when I'm ready,' he said, with a firmness that communicated a deeper message.

On a personal level, his life was also changing. His relationship with Mariella, who perhaps hoped he would retire once his first World Championship was secure, faded away after he fell head over heels for Marlene Knaus, a former girlfriend of actor Curt Jurgens. Born in Venezuela, she and what Niki described as her 'marvellously chaotic' family lived on the Mediterranean island of Ibiza and the World Champion was captivated. Their somewhat furtive courtship was aided by the fact that Lauda had by now taken to the air in his own Cessna Golden Eagle, and they married in the spring of 1976. It was destined to be a volatile, slightly barmy relationship, but 13 years later they remain together. 'When I married Marlene the first things I lost were all my sweaters, the second thing my Range Rover,' reflects Niki.

At the start of that year Lauda won in Brazil, and again in South Africa, rounding off the 312T's career with second place to the hard-charging Regazzoni at Long Beach. For the Spanish GP, Ferrari fielded an uprated version of the car – dubbed the 'T2' – the most obvious change on which was ducting down either side of the cockpit to channel air to the engine, the tall airboxes of the previous few seasons having been outlawed by a change in the regulations.

Prior to that Járama race Niki had cracked two ribs when a tractor rolled over on him in the grounds of his lakeside home near Salzburg. In considerable

Top: *Niki receives the winner's trophy at Kyalami from past champion Jackie Stewart.*

Above: *Niki chatting with a grimacing Bernie Ecclestone and the debonair Huschke von Hanstein, 1976 Monaco Grand Prix.*

Friends and soul-mates. Some people were surprised at the firm friendship that grew up between the emotional, extrovert James Hunt and the cool, pragmatic Lauda. But they got on enormously well and formed something of a mutual admiration society for each other's talents.

Overleaf: Lauda's Ferrari 312 T2 leads Hunt's McLaren and Clay Regazzoni's T2 in the opening stages of the restarted 1976 British GP. James beat Niki across the line, but FISA eventually awarded Lauda the win after Hunt's participation in the second start was deemed illegal.

pain, he duly planted the T2 on pole position at Járama and led initially, only to be overtaken by Hunt's McLaren which went on to win. James was subsequently disqualified when his M23's rear track was adjudged a fraction too wide, so Niki took the victory after all.

More wins followed at Monaco and Zolder, plus a hard-earned third place in the Swedish GP behind the two Tyrrell six-wheelers of Jody Scheckter and Patrick Depailler. Behind the scenes, however, Niki could detect a worrying inclination towards taking things easy. Lauda found it difficult to make the point to Audetto that Ferrari's success was a direct result of the enormous amount of testing that had been carried out over the previous couple of seasons. Slowly, almost imperceptibly, he could feel the team's momentum slipping away. Too many people were being tricked into believing the old chestnut 'anybody can win in a Ferrari...'

Hunt had signalled that he would be Niki's most formidable opposition as early as Brazil when he put the M23 on pole position – and James was there waiting to inherit victory in the French GP when Niki's Ferrari broke its crankshaft. Then came Brands Hatch, the first-corner collision, the much-publicised restart, the controversy over James's presence on the grid and his eventual victory over Niki in the race. In some ways it hardly mattered that James would later be disqualified, the FIA Court of Appeal ruling that he was ineligible to take the restart because he was not actually running at the moment the red flag was shown. More importantly, he had made the point that Lauda was going to have to fight him all the way for the World Championship.

Sunday, 1 August 1976 was the single most significant day in the life of Niki Lauda, professional racing driver. The ripple effects of his accident at the Nürburgring in the German Grand Prix had implications which would, directly and obliquely, affect his life for the next decade. In the first place, it has to be remembered that the '76 German Grand Prix took place against a backdrop of debate and concern over the suitability of the Nürburgring *Nordschleife* as a venue for World Championship Grand Prix motor racing.

Lauda's involvement in all this is quite straightforward yet, in the wake of his accident, a tangle of half-truths, inaccuracies and blatant distortion has 'fingered' the Austrian as being solely responsible for the track's demise. The momentum of these inaccuracies is such that it is hard for the truth of the matter to overtake the lies. But, for the record, the facts are as follows.

The drivers' real concern about the Nürburgring stemmed not from its challenge as a Grand Prix circuit, but from the difficulty in marshalling it as securely as a shorter, more accessible track. Although Lauda had broken a wrist

when his BRM crashed at the Bergwerk corner in 1973 – a few hundred yards from the scene of his 1976 accident – this had not prejudiced him unduly against the circuit, as many of his critics have suggested. In putting forward a selective argument against Niki's standpoint, they had deliberately to overlook the fact that he'd started from pole position in 1975, and the following year lined up a mere 0.9s slower than Hunt's pole position McLaren.

It was depressingly overcast and wet for the start of the 1976 race, only McLaren number two driver Jochen Mass starting on slicks after being tipped that the track was drying fast away from the start/finish area. By the end of the second lap he was leading by a mile, literally – but then the red flag came out and the race was stopped.

Having started on rain tyres, Lauda pitted at the end of the opening lap and rejoined at the tail of the field. He was cutting through the ranks of slower cars by the time he reached the Adenau bridge section, but his Ferrari never made it as far as the Bergwerk right-hander. In an accident witnessed by only a handful of people, and recorded by a 15-year-old spectator on home movie film, the Ferrari 312T2 went violently out of control on a fast left-hand bend, shooting through the catch-fencing on the right and smashing into a rock face, from where it bounced back, in flames, into the middle of the road.

The wrecked Ferrari was then hit by Brett Lunger's Surtees TS16, the impact wrenching off Niki's helmet, and he was extricated from the wreckage thanks to the selfless efforts of the American driver, Guy Edwards, a track marshal and – in particular – Arturo Merzario, who plunged into the flames to release Lauda's seat harness. He was quickly removed to hospital by helicopter where his life hung by a frail thread for several days, his most serious problem being the effects of inhaling toxic fumes from the Ferrari's burning glass-fibre bodywork.

At one point he received the last rites of the Roman Catholic church – and that frightened him so much that he almost leapt from his sick bed with indignation. Whatever else might happen, he was determined that he wasn't about to die, and from then on his physical recovery proceeded at a remarkable pace. He had suffered unpleasant burns to the top of his face and one ear remains badly disfigured to this day, but Niki shrugged the psychological effects of the accident aside with remarkable stoicism.

It is generally accepted that a rear suspension failure caused the accident, as

*Trouble brewing as Niki's 312T2, wearing deep-grooved
rain tyres, slithers around midfield at the Nürburgring
just after the start. Ahead of him is Ronnie Peterson's
March 761, while Alan Jones's Surtees TS19 is lurching
along the grass, abreast of Carlos Reutemann's Brabham
BT45 and Gunnar Nilsson's Lotus 77.*

evidenced by the fact that the car spun with its tail out to the left as it plunged off the road on the fast left-hand kink. Had Niki just lost control, natural centrifugal forces would have sent it pirouetting with its tail out to the right.

Ferrari, predictably, was thrown into utter and complete confusion after Lauda's accident. As James Hunt continued to gobble up Niki's championship points advantage, the Maranello management ran seven ways at once, first trying to get Ronnie Peterson out of his March contract, then signing Carlos Reutemann who switched from Brabham at the end of August. It was just as well that Niki had a contract in his pocket for 1977 as few people at Ferrari had much confidence that he would be any good behind the wheel after his shocking experience.

Niki was now up against it in a big way. He'd always had a remarkably intimate relationship with Enzo Ferrari, the Commendatore indulging the Austrian's candour, which was always spiced with a degree of over-familiarity that might have proved suicidal for any other driver's career prospects. The way in which Niki negotiated his contract details with the Old Man was amazing, to say the least. Through Ferrari's illegitimate son, Piero Lardi, Niki would lay down outrageous demands which had Ferrari bellowing at him in indignation, accusing his number one driver of being a 'jew boy' and threatening to fire him. Niki just thought it was all a good laugh...

Forcing the pace of his recovery, Lauda appeared again in time for the Italian Grand Prix at Monza just over two months later. His head swathed in blood-soaked bandages beneath his helmet, this remarkable little man drove his Ferrari to fourth place on his comeback drive, behind Peterson's March, Regazzoni's 312T2 and Jacques Laffite's Ligier JS5, recording second-fastest lap of the race in the process.

Sadly, by the end of that weekend, he had begun to understand what he was up against in his quest to keep hold of the World Championship. Ferrari's test and development programme had all but collapsed and Hunt retained the upper hand as the season drew to its close, storming his McLaren to brilliant victories at Mosport Park and Watkins Glen, despite the disappointment of hearing that the FIA had finally deprived him of the Brands Hatch victory.

At the end of the day, of course, James was to win the championship by taking a nail-biting third place in the Japanese GP at Mount Fuji. The race started on an almost flooded track and Lauda, who'd qualified third, took the objective

Top: *Looking thoughtful and somewhat forlorn,
answering questions from journalist friend Heinz Prüller
in the pits at Monza, 1976.*

Above: *Wheel to wheel with Vittorio Brambilla's March
761 during his magnificent comeback drive at Monza,
1976. Niki finished fourth with second-fastest race
lap to his credit.*

decision to withdraw on the second lap. His relationship with Enzo Ferrari was never quite the same again.

Lauda has never wavered about his decision to withdraw from that race. 'Alright, so everything dried out towards the end and James was World Champion. But people tend to forget how bad those conditions were. Alright, nothing happened. Hunt was champion and Lauda, the idiot, pulled out. But if something tragic had happened, if something had gone wrong with James's pit stop and he'd lost a few more seconds, if, say, somebody had been killed.... If I'd been champion, then everybody would have been dancing round saying "Lauda, he's a genius, he's fantastic, what a tactician...". And it would have all been sheer nonsense, nothing to do with reality.'

Almost as if he had to be punished, Niki found himself pointedly left out of almost all the team's test programmes, Ferrari's efforts now apparently being firmly focused on Carlos Reutemann. The Argentinian driver, whom most people found deep, thoughtful and fundamentally very likeable, sparked a most unusual reaction from his team-mate. Niki quickly made up his mind that he couldn't stand the sight of him, a reaction that was almost out of character for the normally placid, usually objective Austrian. The tone of their relationship could be summed up from Niki's classic response to the question: 'Do you regard Reutemann as a team-mate or a rival?' Niki replied immediately, 'Neither...'

After Reutemann triumphed in the Brazilian GP at Interlagos, Niki managed to swing the entire team's efforts back behind him, bouncing back into the headlines with a fine victory in the South African GP. Yet it was a success tinged with sadness, for Tom Pryce had been killed in a bizarre collision with a marshal and debris from the Welshman's wrecked Shadow punctured both the oil and water radiators on the winning Ferrari. Niki had managed to nurse the car home to the chequered flag with all his old sympathetic flair and sensitivity.

Two more victories followed in 1977, at Hockenheim and Zandvoort, and Niki Lauda managed to regain his World Championship with a fourth place at Watkins Glen, with two races still to run. By then, though, he had decided he wanted out and had signed a contract to drive for Bernie Ecclestone's Brabham team in 1978, tantalised by the prospect of the new Gordon Murray-designed 'surface cooling' Brabham BT46. He quit with two races to go, infuriated over the small-minded way in which Ferrari had fired his mechanic Ermanno

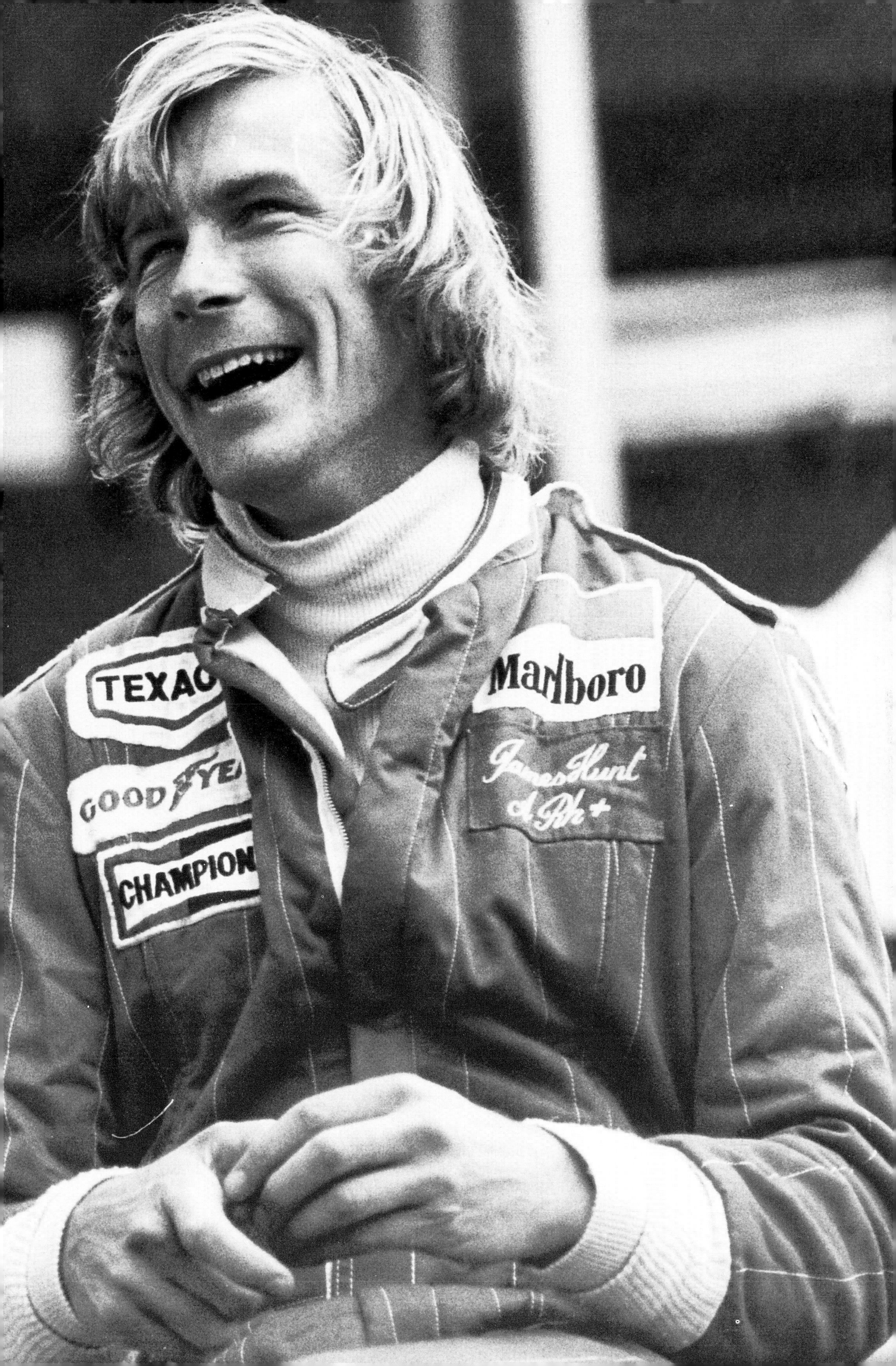
TEXACO
GOODYEAR
CHAMPION
Marlboro
James Hunt

Fourth place in the rain-soaked United States GP at Watkins Glen was sufficient for Niki to clinch the 1977 World Championship. He quit Ferrari immediately afterwards, declining to take part in the last two races of the season.

Cuoghi after he had indicated he would be following his driver to Brabham.

Niki rationalised his decision to leave Ferrari quite straightforwardly: 'One morning I just found myself not feeling about Ferrari as I had in the past. Like painters, we racing drivers have an artistic inclination and are individualists. Our task is to have a free head, come to a race and do more than normal people can manage. But it became like being married to a bad woman. If you're in that situation then you haven't got a clear head, you can't give of your best.

'I worked hard this year with the team. I had always been prepared to give 110 per cent effort to Ferrari, but to do that you've got to be in a very happy situation. You might work all night, for example, for an employer whom you like and get on well with. If you have a normal job, without this special relationship, you simply take the attitude "well, it's five past five, time to go home". In this business you need to have an extremely good relationship with the person you are driving for.

'As far as Enzo Ferrari was concerned, things began to change this year. Political problems, aggravation, the Italian press....In the past I'd have done anything he wanted me to do, but suddenly my freedom seemed to have gone and I didn't want to do much more than normal.'

Optimistically, he looked forward to the fresh challenge of driving for Brabham, but his excitement over the new Alfa-engined BT46 wildly outstripped the car's capability to deliver results. His enthusiasm seemed almost irrational.

'One day I went to England to negotiate with Bernie. We spent an afternoon talking about my contract, how we would get the money together. Then he said, "Come outside, I've got something to show you..." And there it was. The BT46, complete and ready to go. I was so excited that if Bernie had said, "Look, give me £10 and you can drive that car" I would have said, "here is £10". That's when I realised I wanted to drive it so badly.

'So I think logically about Gordon Murray. All his cars have been fast from the word go – the BT42, BT44, BT44B and the BT45. He's not just good, he's fantastic. Each car has been an excellent machine. Normally a new car is difficult and you've got lots of work to do. I reckon the BT46 must be as good as it looks. So then you say, "OK, but it's not reliable", but what is reliability? It's the easiest thing in the world. Just run the car. Get the thing working, look at it logically. Perhaps, for example, the brake pedal is going soft. There's no point in just accepting it. Get it working properly.'

In retrospect, it seems remarkably simplistic stuff from such a pragmatist and Niki was destined to be disappointed in the level of mechanical reliability produced by the Brabham-Alfa combination. The first disappointment came, of

*Youthful and optimistic, photographed in 1972 during his
season driving for the STP March team in F1 and F2.*

Above: *Heading for second place behind Dave Morgan's Brabham in the 1972 Formula 2 season opener at Mallory Park.*

The March 721G, seen here during the French G at Clermont-Ferrand (right), was an improvement on the drea 'X' but all the team's eff were concentrated on Ronnie Peterson.

Right: *Wrestling the troublesome March 721X round Járama during practice for the Spanish GP. Niki ended the weekend wondering whether he could drive after all.*

Below: *Niki scored his first World Championship points
in the 1973 Belgian GP at Zolder, his only top-six finish
with the BRM.*

Top right: *Niki with BRM designer Mike Pilbeam in
the pits at Kyalami, 1973.*

Leading the Canadian GP (opposite) *with the BRM
P160. Gearbox problems eventually put an end to that
fine performance.*

*Left: Heading for his first GP victory: keeping the Ferrari
B3 under control at slippery Járama.*

*Niki with Mauro Forghieri. He admired the Italian
designer's genius but found him temperamental
to work with.*

Above: *Ahead at Monaco. Niki scored the first of his two
victories through the streets of the Principality
with the 312 T in 1975.*

Opposite: *Practising for the 1976 German GP at the old Nürburgring, the event that changed his life…*

Above: *Clinching that 1975 World Championship with a well-judged run to third place at Monza, behind Regazzoni and Fittipaldi.*

*Hunt and Lauda: good friends off the track, but fierce
rivals for the 1976 World Championship.*

*Brave man. Niki's Ferrari 312 T2 (above) on its way to
fourth place in the 1976 Italian GP only two months after
he had received the last rites.*

He went that-away…Niki doing his disappearing act at Anderstorp in the 1978 Swedish GP at the wheel of the Brabham BT46 'fan-car'.

Back in the old routine. Third race back, first win for
McLaren – on top at Long Beach, 1982.

Above right: *Established star greets future ace.*
Celebrating Ayrton Senna's third place for Toleman after
Niki had won the '84 British GP for McLaren.

Below right: *Sweet moment. Victory at last in Austria*
as Niki's McLaren, gearbox almost destroyed, crosses the
line to win the '84 race.

Title number three. Taking the chequered flag (left) at Estoril, 1984, where Niki clinched his third World Championship.

Lauda with Prost, in 1984. Between them, the two men won 12 of the season's 16 races and a firm bond developed between them.

course, when the surface cooling system had to be abandoned and the advent of Colin Chapman's ground-effect aerodynamics made it necessary for Murray, handicapped by the width of the Alfa flat-12 engine, to seek a technical solution which would allow him to match the prodigious downforce being developed by the Lotus 78. The result was the 'fan car', which Niki used to win the 1978 Swedish GP at Anderstorp before the system was subsequently outlawed by FISA.

All things taken into account, Niki's relationship with the Brabham team was enjoyable, but unproductive. He inherited victory in the Italian GP only when Andretti and Villeneuve were penalised for jump starts and, by the end of the 1978 season, one could sense that his ambition was becoming slightly blunted. In 1979, also, he would face yet another challenge.

Throughout 1978 Niki's partner had been John Watson, the genial, easy-going Ulsterman who'd joined the team from Penske at the start of 1977. But as John came to appreciate, Niki was much more to Bernie Ecclestone's taste as far as personality was concerned.

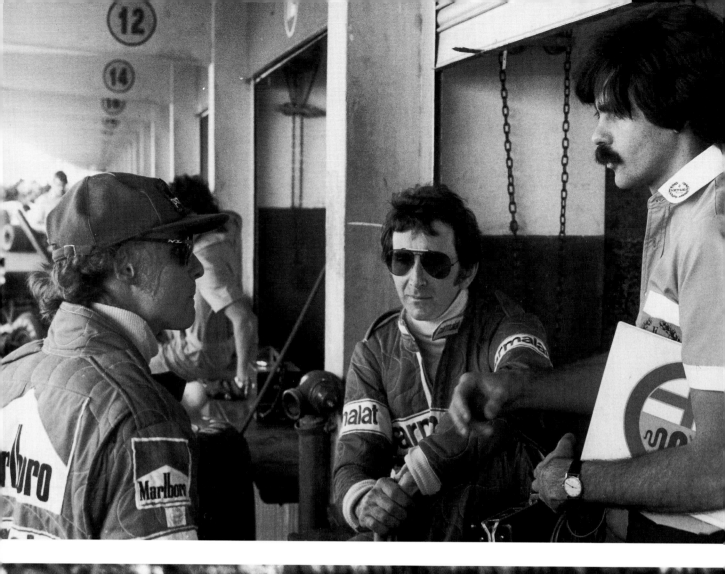

'I had no problems at all with my relationship with either of them,' reflected Watson. 'It was fantastic working with Niki and we had more laughs and fun with each other than either of us had experienced with a team-mate before. But I always felt that Bernie seemed to like people with a more aggressive nature than I'd got. I was no less ambitious than Niki behind the wheel, but I certainly wasn't as aggressive as him out of the cockpit in everyday life.'

Watson's place in the Brabham line-up went to the gifted Brazilian newcomer, Nelson Piquet, the dominant force on the 1978 British F3 scene. Clearly a man with potential, he was destined to keep Niki dancing on his toes for much of 1979.

Gordon Murray insisted that Alfa Romeo build a V12 engine in order that he could complete a proper ground-effect chassis design for 1979, and while Alfa responded magnificently, completing the new engine in six months, the BT48 chassis took some time for the drivers to master. And Niki was under pressure.

In the South African GP, Lauda and Piquet finished 6–7. Niki was impressed. 'Every time I looked in my mirrors, there was Nelson. So I tried hard for a couple of laps, looked again and he was still there, right behind...' It proved, however, to be a long, frustrating summer. The Alfa V12s were not only unreliable, their performance varied horrendously from engine to engine. Behind the scenes, Niki opened negotiations which might have led to his driving a McLaren-BMW turbo. They came to nothing. He would have to wait another three years before he forged a partnership with McLaren.

Piquet: 'There were times that I was quicker than Niki in practice during 1979 and just came in, got out and sat on the pit wall to watch. He would be out there pounding round, trying absolutely as hard as he could, but there was just no way he could match my times. If you had a bad engine, you were uncompetitive. It was as straightforward as that.'

Ironically, after struggling through an unproductive summer of World Championship races, Niki bagged victory in the non-title Gran Premio Dino Ferrari, staged at the refurbished Imola circuit a week after the Italian GP. By then Ecclestone and Murray had taken the decision to drop the overweight, thirsty Alfa V12 and initiated an intensive programme to build three Cosworth-engined BT49s in time for the Canadian GP. But, by then, Niki had his sights set on retirement.

His enthusiasm for aviation now took over. Although in the early 1970s he'd

confessed to being 'scared stiff' after taking a trip in a single-engined trainer, he soon shrugged aside that early apprehension and became increasingly obsessed by flying. After a couple of Cessna Golden Eagles, he had a Citation jet (which he sold to Nelson Piquet), a Learjet, a Falcon 10, a Falcon 20, then back to a Learjet again. In 1978 he started Lauda-air as a small charter airline using a twin turboprop Fokker F27 and had grandiose plans to expand into the charter market. With that in mind, a deposit was placed on a McDonnell-Douglas DC-10.

Practice at Montreal produced a major surprise when, after only ten laps in the BT49, Niki pulled into the pits to announce that he wanted to quit. There and then. Rather than persuade him to think about it, Bernie Ecclestone wisely said, 'OK, if you want to go, then I agree it's best to go now.' Within hours he had returned to his hotel and jetted off to the McDonnell-Douglas factory in California. 'I was no longer getting any pleasure from driving round and round in circles. I feel I have better things to do with my life,' he explained.

Why did he do it? People have speculated that he was getting bored, losing his touch and knew full well that Piquet could run rings round him. Alan Jones, then reaching the peak of his career with Williams, came up with the daft hypothesis that Niki realised, with Brabham returning to the Cosworth route, that it would just be too much like hard work to keep up. In truth, it was necessary to take Niki's words at face value. He'd simply become bored. But, although even he didn't know it at the time, he was merely taking an extended pause for breath...

Above left: *Sensational victory. Niki at speed in the*
Brabham BT46 'fan-car' with which he blitzed the
opposition to win the Swedish GP at Anderstorp.

Left: *All the opposition saw of Gordon Murray's latest*
brain child...

Above: *On the brink of retirement. Niki with the new*
BT49-Cosworth DFV during first practice for the 1979
Canadian GP at Montreal. Shortly after this picture was
taken, he pulled into the pits and told Bernie Ecclestone
he was going to quit...

A more familiar sight in 1979 was Niki, helmet in hand,
walking back to the pits after his Brabham-Alfa
had expired.

It had certainly been fun while it lasted. He had won two World Championships, and provided us all with plenty of wry humour and timely one-liners. The world of Grand Prix racing got on with its own business, with Alan Jones winning the 1980 championship and Nelson Piquet the 1981 title. Meanwhile, the aviation world had been hard hit by the prevailing worldwide financial recession and Lauda-air was no exception. Niki's company had been forced to cancel its option on that DC-10 and had experienced trouble from the state-run Austrian Airlines when it came to obtaining route licences.

When he was invited to test a McLaren MP4 at Donington Park towards the end of 1981, it became clear that Ron Dennis, then Commercial Director of McLaren International, and Marlboro's John Hogan were on the verge of a major coup. In 1979 Lauda had driven a BMW M1 entered by Dennis, and sponsored by Marlboro, in the Grand Prix-supporting Pro-Car series. Sure enough, in October 1981 the announcement was made. Niki Lauda would return to drive alongside John Watson for 1982.

Memories seemed to blur slightly. Had he retired at the end of 1979? Or had he really been racing all along – and we'd just not noticed. It was impossible to believe that he'd been gone for more than two years. Back into the F1 arena he strode, toothy smile and Parmalat cap advertising his arrival. Wry grin, gently nodding head, all the old jokes. It was if he had been kept in some sort of time capsule, preserved in amber for the moment he would return to the sport that had made him a hero.

But why? Niki: 'For two years, I didn't take any real interest in motor racing. It was a chapter in my life I believed was over. My interest was now flying and it absorbed me, totally. I could watch a Grand Prix start and feel not even the slightest tremble of excitement or enthusiasm. I would think "what's that all about?" and turn away. It wasn't until I went to the 1981 Austrian GP and suddenly found myself thinking "I wonder..."

'Once I'd made the decision to come back, the rest was easy. OK, so I had a few fleeting doubts when I did that Donington test for the first time, but it was my own fault in a way. I'd put myself in a new car, on a track I'd never seen before, on radial tyres which I'd never tried before. But the worry soon passed. By the end of the day, I reckoned I could do it.'

Using the same rational approach he'd previously attempted to apply to the business of car testing, Niki applied similar logic to the question of revitalising

his personal fitness. With the assistance of Willi Dungl, the ski-training guru who'd helped him conquer the side-effects of the Nürburgring accident, he mapped out a gruelling programme of physical rehabilitation.

'Getting fit is simple and straightforward,' asserts Niki. 'All you have to do is to run for ten minutes today, thirty minutes tomorrow and an hour the next day. Run, run, run...train, train, train...and you're fit. There's nothing easier in the world, once you've taken the mental decision to do it.' His pragmatist approach could be infuriating at times...

Niki's 1982 season produced a victory in his third race – Long Beach – and a second triumph at Brands Hatch. Indeed, he was a contender from day one, finishing fourth in his comeback race at Kyalami. By the time he came to the French GP at Paul Ricard, Ron Dennis was sufficiently impressed to describe him as 'the best driver in the car, and the best driver out of the car. That doesn't mean he's got to be winning all the time, or be the fastest man out on the track. But he has a total commitment to what he is doing and – as long as the team is behind him – that means results. We provide the ingredients, and Niki mixes the cake.'

He was perhaps more streetwise as well. His starkly realistic streak remained well to the fore, but many people recognised that his wider business experience had brought a mellow, even more philosophical, slant to his character. But he was still enormously shrewd.

Prior to the start of the season, he was glancing through the FISA super licence form when it struck him that its wording effectively gave *carte blanche* to the team owners to decide which driver drove when, and for whom. 'I thought that was crazy,' he explained, 'so I rang up Didier Pironi (then President of the GPDA) and drew it to his attention. He told me it was all fine, not to worry. So I said "Look, I don't know where you're from, but I'm an Austrian and I'm telling you this is all shit." I tried to explain all the implied consequences and he began to understand. I gave him an example of what might happen; under the terms of this licence, if I'd fallen out with McLaren and got the sack, I would find it almost impossible to get another drive unless they agreed.'

What stemmed from all this was the drivers' strike at Kyalami in 1982. Cynics might suggest that Niki loaded the gun and got Pironi to pull the trigger...

That first season back also reminded us of the caring and concerned side of

*Niki scored a memorable British GP victory at Brands
Hatch, six years after his controversial triumph for
Ferrari. Didier Pironi, whose Ferrari finished second,
looked less than delighted as they posed together
on the rostrum.*

his nature. And of his stature. While many of his contemporaries were attempting to shrug off Gilles Villeneuve's fatal crash at Zolder as just another racing accident, Niki blamed Jochen Mass for causing the disaster. Some of the half-baked brigade among the sport's hierarchy believed Lauda should have been reprimanded for this outburst, but fortunately they thought better of it. Nothing was said.

Niki's philosophical side reflected his dismay at the uncaring, shrug-it-aside indifference that ran through F1 like a stick of rock. 'Villeneuve dies and we come to North America a few weeks later and nobody talks about him,' he said quietly. 'I think that's bloody sad. Life moves too quickly. Sixteen Grands Prix, another race, another winner. The only thing a driver can do is to close himself off from the atmosphere, concentrate on his own line. Decide what you are going to do, and then stick to your principles.'

He found it difficult to rationalise how his spell in retirement had changed his personal credo. 'Perhaps I'm a little more open with people. In the past I've always been building mental walls around myself, attempting to protect myself from all the pressure. Now the walls are down. I'm relaxed, perhaps easier to get on with. But I sometimes feel claustrophobic, vulnerable, open...as if I might get hurt personally. Almost as though I'm expecting somebody to kick me in the teeth.'

It wasn't a bad year, 1982. By his own admission, he screwed up what should have been a relatively straightforward victory at Detroit, trying too hard while forgetting that the race had been restarted and was therefore an aggregate affair. 'If I'd stayed within five seconds of Watson I would have won by seven seconds, because I was twelve seconds ahead of him when the first part was stopped. But I forgot completely about the first race. I took the second race as one race on its own. All that was in my mind was to pass Watson...' In this frantic frame of mind, he collided with Keke Rosberg's Williams and had to retire. Watson went on to win.

He finished 1982 fifth in the World Championship, 14 points behind winner Rosberg. Watson continued to partner him through a barren 1983 season in which John scored the sole McLaren success, at Long Beach. But there was a brand new engine in prospect, for Ron Dennis and the team's Technical Director, John Barnard, had forged a splendidly ambitious deal with Porsche for the manufacture of an all-new, state-of-the-art, 1½-litre turbo V6 engine. With sponsorship from TAG, the Franco-Saudi high technology corporation, the TAG turbo first ran in the 1983 Dutch GP at Zandvoort. Installed in a McLaren MP4/1E test car, Lauda was at the wheel.

At the end of 1983, Renault fired Alain Prost. The French driver was made the scapegoat for the team's abysmal failure to win the World Championship, but McLaren quickly snapped him up at a bargain basement price. Suddenly Niki found himself with a major challenge on his hands from within his 'own' team. But what followed was probably the most remarkable demonstration of team togetherness in recent Grand Prix history. The superb TAG-engined McLaren MP4/2s won 12 of the season's 16 races, and although this record was topped by Senna and Prost with their Honda-engined cars four years later, the Lauda-Prost partnership must be adjudged the more remarkable of the two. Unlike the situation in 1988, once certain initial reservations – bred out of mutual caution – were swept aside, the two men got on with each other like a house on fire.

Niki started out in circumspect mood. 'I'm just the driver,' he snapped. 'It's not my team. So now comes Mr Prost to McLaren. Sure I work with him...he seems like a sensible guy.'

By contrast, Alain opened on a more enthusiastic note. 'In my karting days,' he explained, 'Niki was my idol. I modelled myself on him and dreamed of achieving his success. Now here I am in the same team, with the same equipment, the same chances...'

Make no mistake, Niki had enjoyed the situation with good old Wattie as his team-mate. It wasn't so important that John could sometimes beat him, for Niki always believed that he had something of a psychological advantage over the Ulsterman. But Prost was an unknown who would, quite clearly, take some handling. Watson effectively echoed those sentiments. 'The thing about having Niki in a team is that it doesn't matter what's written on a contract, or how the team is basically run. Niki will assume what he wants to assume. He'll take his own position.' Prost's arrival seriously threatened that *modus operandi*.

If truth be told, the McLaren team really wanted Prost to take the 1984 championship. He represented their hopes and aspirations for the future. Unkindly, it was felt that another World Championship for Lauda...well, it would be just that. Another feather in the Austrian's cap, a variation on the 'anybody can win in a Ferrari' theme. Niki Lauda could win World Championships in anybody's car.

It was a strange paradox that Ron Dennis, the man whose master stroke it had been to lure Niki from retirement, started to become strangely uncomfortable about the amount of attention that was centring on the Austrian. Back in 1982 he'd hedged his bets with a clause in Lauda's contract to the effect that, if he was demonstrably not up to the job, he could be replaced after four races. Typically, Niki's confidence was such that he readily accepted the deal.

By 1984, however, Dennis was locked into the second year of an extremely expensive contract with Niki and began showing signs of resenting how little public credit was being given for his, the team's and (notably) for designer John Barnard's efforts. In retrospect, Niki could probably have defused this tension with a little effort, but he wouldn't have any truck with what he saw as an unnecessary upwelling of temperament.

The battle for the championship was virtually a two-horse race from the start, with the combination of these two great drivers, a superb chassis and engine, plus McLaren International's near-faultless preparation seeing off most of the opposition on Michelin rubber. Elio de Angelis's Goodyear-shod Lotus 95T-Renault chased hard in third place, but remained a mathematical outside contender until the end of August only through praiseworthy consistency amid the supporting cast.

Prost kicked off with a psychologically crucial maiden victory at Rio; Niki came back with a fine win at Kyalami, but only after Alain was forced to swap to the spare car on the grid and start from the pit lane. When Alboreto scored a lucky win at Zolder for Ferrari, the McLarens both retired early, but thereafter the McLaren team only lost at Dallas (where Rosberg won for Williams) plus Detroit and Montreal (where the grenade-like BMW engine in Piquet's Brabham BT53 survived the distance).

Strangely, they seldom managed to get locked into combat at the front of the field, although Niki chased Alain home at Hockenheim and Zandvoort, disappointed that his wrong tyre strategy at the latter race prevented him from genuinely challenging in the closing stages. Lauda's luck was quite remarkable, though. They flipped a coin for their race engines at Monza; Alain's blew up, Niki won. At Brands Hatch, Alain's gearbox wilted, Niki won again.

At the Österreichring Alain spun out on oil dumped by de Angelis as he struggled to hold his McLaren in gear. Niki took the lead, then heard a sharp report from his gearbox. Clearly a gear had broken up. Stirring the lever round

in order to limp back to the pits, he found the transmission still functioned – after a fashion. He kept going to such good effect that Piquet, running second, threw in the towel and cruised home for six points. 'If you'd have challenged me, there would have been no way to keep you back,' he told the flabbergasted Brazilian as they strolled to the winner's rostrum.

Niki's capacity as a poker player was stretched to the limit towards the end of the summer when he agreed a deal for 1985 with the Renault team, stimulated by the prospect of yet another fresh challenge. Unfortunately team-manager Gérard Larrousse turned the negotiations into a French farce when it transpired that he wasn't ultimately authorised to clinch the terms of the contract. Then Ron Dennis found out what he was up to. Niki was in a corner. He had to stay with McLaren for '85, but Ron had the whip hand when it came to negotiating terms. But, even with the odds stacked against him, Niki canvassed Marlboro's intervention to increase his retainer to what he considered a realistic level. It was a dangerous game, for Dennis at one point threatened to sign Senna as a replacement if Lauda didn't complete the deal.

In the end, the 1984 championship battle all came down to the last race of the year, the Portuguese GP at Estoril. Alain did everything one could have expected of him, leading from start to finish. But it wasn't enough. When Nigel Mansell's Lotus 95T ran out of brakes and relinquished second place, Niki moved up to take six crucial points. His third World Championship was in the bag by the wafer-thin margin of half a point. 'Don't worry about it,' he told a tearful Prost, 'next year the title will be yours...' He was right there, too.

Prost: 'I was happy that Niki stayed on with us in 1985. OK, he won the championship and I didn't. I can live with that. What was important was the trust between us. I didn't know Niki very well when I came to McLaren – it's not easy to know him well. But I believed he was completely honest and, by

98

the end of the season, I was certain.'

Keke Rosberg, grappling with the first generation Williams-Honda throughout 1984, reckoned Niki had been trying desperately hard all through that summer. 'He's had Prost so big in his eyes. I've been with Niki in a few corners and I've been given a very clear picture; either I move, or something's going to happen. Clean – but absolutely uncompromising.'

Niki, quite simply, described it as the most satisfying season he had ever known. 'I'd never been in this position with a team-mate before. I had to drive faster and faster, better and better, all the time to have a chance of competing with him.'

As a tailpiece to that remarkable season, McLaren quickly realised that they had two star drivers who could absolutely be relied upon to bring the cars home in one piece – to the point where they stopped bothering to insure the chassis, so confident had they become.

For John Barnard, from an engineer's standpoint, 1984 had provided a fascinating insight into the two men's capabilities. 'Niki was a good development driver alright,' he admits, 'but sometimes he definitely wasn't as good as Alain. The problem could be that he was such a strong-minded person. If you clicked with him in the same direction he was an immovable force. But sometimes I felt he was too quick to reach a conclusion during testing, whereas Alain took longer to be sure. With Niki, there could be no misunderstanding. It was either this or that.'

Goodyear's Racing Manager, Lee Gaug, agreed. 'He always wanted a firm decision on what tyres to race from the start of a race. He hated uncertainty and didn't like improvising in the sense that he didn't want to make a decision about whether or not to make a tyre stop once the race had started. Alain was more flexible in this respect.'

But, as Barnard is quick to point out, that unshakable, ultra-positive nature could be of enormous benefit. 'It would help push through programmes, particularly with Porsche on the TAG turbo project,' he recalls. 'Porsche always listened to him – and believed him. He had their ear, no question about it...'

Top: *'Zat's it. Finish! Thank you and goodbye…' Niki
announces his impending retirement at the ill-starred
Austrian GP press conference. The disapproving Ron
Dennis is about to make a tactical* faux pas…

Above: *Last win: Zandvoort, 1985, and Niki gives
Alain some tuition in Formula Ford driving tactics as he
heads for victory in the Dutch GP.*

POSTSCRIPT

After that fairy-tale ending to 1984, Niki Lauda's racing achievement plummeted in 1985. As Prost duly headed towards his expected first World Championship title, so Niki became less assertive when it came to wringing out a single, high-boost qualifying lap from his McLaren-TAG. He also had some bitterly bad luck, notching up retirement after retirement for no obvious reason. It was as if he knew his lucky streak had come to an end. Except that he didn't believe in luck.

He announced his retirement at the Österreichring, scene of his remarkable triumph 12 months before. He also had a major falling-out with Ron Dennis over the manner of that announcement, Niki convening a Marlboro-staged press conference without consulting his team boss. Dennis considered it to be a breach of etiquette. Niki told him not to be so daft. Ron also made an ill-timed outburst to the effect that the real person Niki should be thanking for his success was John Barnard. Later Ron would concede that he could have timed things rather better.

One glorious moment remained. Thanks to Prost being delayed over-long in a Zandvoort tyre stop, he emerged from the pits to find himself behind Lauda on the circuit. But despite gobbling up his lead, Niki pulled every first-year Formula Ford stunt in the book to notch up the twenty-fourth – and last – victory of his career. 'Sure I'll help Alain win the championship if he needs me to,' grinned the toothy old Rat, 'but not just yet...'

As things turned out, his team-mate could manage the task quite nicely by himself, thank you. Fourth place in the Grand Prix of Europe at Brands Hatch – on a day made memorable by Nigel Mansell's first F1 victory – and Alain Prost became the first Frenchman in the sport's history to grasp the world title.

At least Niki could walk away from the sport in the knowledge that he actually led the last Grand Prix of his quite remarkable career. Less satisfying was the way in which that race – the inaugural Australian GP at Adelaide – ended, his McLaren locking a brake and spearing into the wall at the end of the long back straight, in full view of the television cameras.

End of story. Within ten days, he was at Luton airport, undertaking an intensive programme of training to qualify as a Boeing 737 pilot. Three years later, he would come down to Adelaide again for the race. For at least one leg of the 23-hour weekly scheduled service from Vienna to Sydney, via Bangkok, he was in command of a spanking new Lauda-air Boeing 767. Captain Lauda. Just one of 40 such flight deck crew employed by the airline he had founded ten years earlier.

Brushing aside the notion that passengers may travel Lauda-air for the novelty value of perhaps having him in command, the same objective standards of near-perfection which he once applied to his racing technique are now being focused on making Lauda-air one of the most efficient airlines between Europe and Australia. The planes have a central bar area where smoking is permitted and separate toilets for ladies and gentlemen!

'My target is to produce a top quality flight,' he said firmly. 'If that can be done, the rest will follow. If people come off our planes after a bad flight and I'm aboard, they will think: "Hell, why doesn't that man give up flying and go back to motor racing." People want everything to be right. No more than that.'

He draws a valid comparison between motor racing and the airline business. 'All the wheeling and dealing is very much the same,' he grins, 'but with one major difference. The squabbles and disputes among the F1 fraternity are with people you know, in one's own little circus. In the airline business you're fighting the whole world. Taking on governments, battling against conflicting interests where they are all too keen to protect individual rival airlines' business. Believe me, politicians steer aviation, particularly in Europe where it isn't yet a free world as it is in the USA. Sometimes the problems seem so baffling that you don't know where to begin.'

Lauda acknowledges that motor racing put him where he is today. 'It taught me some very good lessons and, sure, I believe my methodical approach helped me enormously. But basically everything I've done stems from motor racing and, as a result, I can honestly thank God that I've got this flying business to keep me occupied. I've dedicated myself to aviation with 150 per cent commitment. You could say I'm trying to be the Ayrton Senna of commercial aviation.'

He signs off with a slice of characteristic wry Lauda humour. 'Flying in itself is nothing special. You push a button in Vienna and the 767 winds up landing in Bangkok 12 hours later. But when something goes wrong, that's when you earn your money...'

NIKI LAUDA · CAREER RECORD
BY JOHN TAYLOR

1968

	Race	Circuit	Date	Entrant	Car	Comment
2c	Bad Mühllacken Hill Climb	Bad Mühllacken	15/04/68	Niki Lauda	Mini Cooper S	2nd in class
1c	Dobratsch Hill Climb	Dobratsch	28/04/68	Niki Lauda	Mini Cooper S	1st in class
1c	Alpl Hill Climb	Alpl	05/05/68	Niki Lauda	Mini Cooper S	1st in class
1c	Engelhartszell Hill Climb	Engelhartszell	26/05/68	Niki Lauda	Mini Cooper S	1st in class
ret	Kasten Hill Climb	Kasten	09/06/68	Niki Lauda	Porsche 911	accident
1c	Koralpe Hill Climb	Koralpe	23/06/68	Niki Lauda	Porsche 911	1st in class
ret	Tulln-Langenlebarn GT Race	Tulln-Langenlebarn	14/07/68	Niki Lauda	Porsche 911	engine
1c	Tauplitzalm Hill Climb	Tauplitzalm	04/08/68	Niki Lauda	Porsche 911	1st in class
1c	Stainz Hill Climb	Stainz	11/08/68	Niki Lauda	Porsche 911	1st in class
1c	Walding Hill Climb	Walding	15/08/68	Niki Lauda	Porsche 911	1st in class
1	Zeltweg GT Race	Zeltweg	25/08/68	Niki Lauda	Porsche 911	1st circuit victory
3	Aspern GT Race	Aspern	06/10/68	Niki Lauda	Porsche 911	
8	Aspern Formula Vee Race	Aspern	06/10/68	Kurt Bergmann Team	Kaimann-Volkswagen	1st single seater drive
ret	Innsbruck GT Race	Innsbruck	13/10/68	Niki Lauda	Porsche 911	reason unknown
1c	Dopplerhütte Hill Climb	Dopplerhütte	27/10/68	Niki Lauda	Porsche 911	1st in class

1969

	Race	Circuit	Date	Entrant	Car	Comment
4	Hockenheim Formula Vee Race	Hockenheim	12/04/69	Kurt Bergmann Team	Kaimann-Volkswagen	
ret	Aspern Formula Vee Race	Aspern	13/04/69	Kurt Bergmann Team	Kaimann-Volkswagen	accident
1	Belgrade Formula Vee Race	Belgrade	20/04/69	Kurt Bergmann Team	Kaimann-Volkswagen	
4	Budapest Formula Vee Race	Budapest	11/05/69	Kurt Bergmann Team	Kaimann-Volkswagen	
5	Rossfeld Hill Climb	Rossfeld	08/06/69	Kurt Bergmann Team	Kaimann-Volkswagen	
2	Hockenheim Formula Vee Race	Hockenheim	15/06/69	Kurt Bergmann Team	Kaimann-Volkswagen	
2	Nürburgring Hansa-Pokal	Nürburgring	29/06/69	Kurt Bergmann Team	Kaimann-Volkswagen	
1	Sopron Formula Vee Race	Sopron	06/06/69	Niki Lauda	Kaimann-Volkswagen	
ret	Tulln-Langenlebarn Saloon Car Race	Tulln-Langenlebarn	13/07/69	Niki Lauda	Opel 1900	engine
3	Tulln-Langenlebarn Formula Vee Race	Tulln-Langenlebarn	13/07/69	Kurt Bergmann Team	Kaimann-Volkswagen	
8	Österreichring Formula Vee Race	Österreichring	27/07/69	Kurt Bergmann Team	Kaimann-Volkswagen	
2	Nürburgring Formula Vee Race	Nürburgring	03/08/69	Kurt Bergmann Team	Kaimann-Volkswagen	
21	Austrian Grand Prix	Österreichring	10/08/69	Otto Stuppacher	Porsche 910	c/d Otto Stuppacher
ret	Mantorp Park Formula Vee Race	Mantorp Park	31/08/69	Kurt Bergmann Team	Kaimann-Volkswagen	fuel pump
3	Salzburgring Formula Vee Race	Salzburgring	21/09/69	Kurt Bergmann Team	Kaimann-Volkswagen	
2	Innsbruck Formula Vee Race	Innsbruck	05/10/69	Kurt Bergmann Team	Kaimann-Volkswagen	
20	Eifel Cup Formula Vee Race	Nürburgring	12/10/69	Kurt Bergmann Team	Kaimann-Volkswagen	
5	Munich-Neibiberg Saloon Car Race	Munich-Neibiberg	26/10/69	Niki Lauda	Opel 1900	
1	Munich-Neibiberg Formula Vee Race	Munich-Niebiberg	26/10/69	Kurt Bergmann Team	Kaimann-Volkswagen	

1970

	Race	Circuit	Date	Entrant	Car	Comment
ret	Nogaro Formula 3 Race	Nogaro	29/03/70	Niki Lauda	McNamara Mk3B-Novamotor	accident
16	Nürburgring Formula 3 Race	Nürburgring	19/04/70	Niki Lauda	McNamara Mk3B-Novamotor	
5	Magny-Cours Formula 3 Race	Magny-Cours	03/05/70	Niki Lauda	McNamara Mk3B-Novamotor	
ret	Hockenheim Formula 3 Race	Hockenheim	10/05/70	Niki Lauda	McNamara Mk3B-Novamotor	accident
6	Österreichring Formula 3 Race	Österreichring	17/05/70	Niki Lauda	McNamara Mk3B-Novamotor	
2	Brno Formula 3 Race	Brno	24/05/70	Niki Lauda	McNamara Mk3B-Novamotor	
dns	Silverstone Formula 3 Race	Silverstone	07/06/70	Niki Lauda	McNamara Mk3B-Novamotor	accident in practice
8	Nuremberg 200	Norisring	28/06/70	Niki Lauda	Porsche 908	
12	Solituderennen	Hockenheim	05/07/70	Niki Lauda	Porsche 908	
5	Hockenheim Formula 3 Race	Hockenheim	05/07/70	Niki Lauda	McNamara Mk3B-Novamotor	
ret	Nürburgring 6 Hours	Nürburgring	12/07/70	Rene Herzog	BMW 1600	reason unknown/c/d Rene Herzog
ret	Shell/Motor Sport Championship Race	Brands Hatch	17/07/70	Niki Lauda	McNamara Mk3B-Novamotor	accident
1	Diepholz Sports Car Race	Diepholz	19/07/70	Niki Lauda	Porsche 908	
5	Karlskoga Formula 3 Race	Karlskoga	09/08/70	Niki Lauda	McNamara Mk3B-Novamotor	
ret	Karlskoga Sports Car Race	Karlskoga	09/08/70	Niki Lauda	Porsche 908	gearbox
ret	Knutstorp Formula 3 Race	Knutstorp	16/08/70	Niki Lauda	McNamara Mk3B-Novamotor	accident
ret	Keimola Interserie Race	Keimola	23/08/70	Niki Lauda	Porsche 908	bearings
4	Zandvoort Formula 3 Race	Zandvoort	30/08/70	Niki Lauda	McNamara Mk3B-Novamotor	
ret	Guards Trophy Formula 3 Race	Brands Hatch	31/08/70	Niki Lauda	McNamara Mk3B-Novamotor	accident
ret	Zolder Formula 3 Race	Zolder	06/09/70	Niki Lauda	McNamara Mk3B-Novamotor	accident
5	Imola 500 KMS	Imola	13/09/70	Niki Lauda	Porsche 908	c/d Freddy Kottulinsky
5	Yellow Pages Trophy	Thruxton	20/09/70	Niki Lauda	Porsche 908	
6	Österreichring 1000 KMS	Österreichring	11/10/70	Niki Lauda	Porsche 908	c/d Peter Peter
3	Nürburgring Sports Car Race	Nürburgring	18/10/70	Niki Lauda	Porsche 908	
1	Martha Grand National	Österreichring	25/10/70	Niki Lauda	Porsche 908	

1971

ret	Speed International Trophy	Mallory Park	14/03/71	March Engineering	March 712M-Cosworth FVA	*fuel pump*
ret	Jim Clark Trophy	Hockenheim	04/04/71	March Engineering	March 712M-Cosworth FVA	*clutch*
10	Jochen Rindt Memorial Trophy	Thruxton	12/04/71	March Engineering	March 712M-Cosworth FVA	
6	Eifelrennen	Nürburgring	02/05/71	March Engineering	March 712M-Cosworth FVA	
7	Madrid Grand Prix	Járama	16/05/71	March Engineering	March 712M-Cosworth FVA	
1	Salzburgring EC Sports Car Race	Salzburgring	23/05/71	Red Rose Racing Team	Chevron B19-Cosworth FVC	
dnq	Hilton Transport Trophy	Crystal Palace	31/05/71	March Engineering	March 712M-Cosworth FVA	
ret	Lottery Grand Prix	Monza	20/06/71	March Engineering	March 712M-Cosworth FVA	*gearbox*
4	Rouen Grand Prix	Rouen	27/06/71	March Engineering	March 712M-Cosworth FVA	
3	Nürburgring 6 Hours	Nürburgring	11/07/71	Alpina Racing Team	BMW 2800CS	*c/d Günther Huber*
ret	Spa 24 Hours	Spa	24/25/07/71	Alpina Racing Team	BMW 2800CS	*c/d Gérard Larrousse*
13	Mantorp Park Grand Prix	Mantorp Park	08/08/71	March Engineering	March 712M-Cosworth FVA	
ret	AUSTRIAN GP	Österreichring	15/08/71	STP March Racing Team	March 711-Cosworth DVF	*handling*
6	Swedish Gold Cup	Kinnekulle	22/08/71	March Engineering	March 712M-Cosworth FVA	
7	Rothmans International Trophy	Brands Hatch	30/08/71	March Engineering	March 712M-Cosworth FVA	
ret	Flugplatzrennen	Tulln-Langenlebarn	01/09/71	March Engineering	March 712M-Cosworth FVA	*accident*
ret	Albi Grand Prix	Albi	26/09/71	March Engineering	March 712M-Cosworth FVA	*reason unknown*
7	Madunina Grand Prix	Vallelunga	10/10/71	March Engineering	March 712M-Cosworth FVA	

1972

11	ARGENTINE GP	Buenos Aires	23/01/72	STP March Racing Team	March 721-Cosworth DFV	
7	SOUTH AFRICAN GP	Kyalami	04/03/72	STP March Racing Team	March 721-Cosworth DFV	
2	John Player Championship Race	Mallory Park	12/03/72	STP March Racing Team	March 722-Ford BDA	
1	John Player Championship Race	Oulton Park	31/03/72	STP March Racing Team	March 722-Ford BDA	
3	Esso Uniflo Trophy Race	Thruxton	03/04/72	STP March Racing Team	March 722-Ford BDA	
ret	Jim Clark Trophy Race	Hockenheim	16/04/72	STP March Racing Team	March 722-Ford BDA	*water pump*
ret	SPANISH GP	Járama	01/05/72	STP March Racing Team	March 721X-Cosworth DFV	*sticking throttle*
ret	Pau Grand Prix	Pau	07/05/72	STP March Racing Team	March 722-Ford BDA	*driveshaft*
16	MONACO GP	Monte Carlo	14/05/72	STP March Racing Team	March 721X-Cosworth DFV	
ret	Brno Grand Prix	Brno	21/05/72	Alpina Racing Team	BMW 2800CS	*engine*
ret	Greater London Trophy Race	Crystal Palace	28/05/72	STP March Racing Team	March 722-Ford BDA	*engine*
12	BELGIAN GP	Nivelles	04/06/72	STP March Racing Team	March 721X-Cosworth DFV	
ret	Jochen Rindt Memorial Trophy	Hockenheim	11/06/72	STP March Racing Team	March 722-Ford BDA	*ignition*
dns	Grand Prix of the Republic	Vallelunga	18/06/72	STP March Racing Team	March 721-Cosworth DFV	*accident in practice*
ret	Rouen Grand Prix	Rouen	25/06/72	STP March Racing Team	March 722-Ford BDA	*engine*
ret	FRENCH GP	Clermont Ferrand	02/07/72	STP March Racing Team	March 721G-Cosworth DFV	*driveshaft*
ret	Jochen Rindt Memorial Trophy	Hockenheim	09/07/72	STP March Racing Team	March 722-Ford BDA	*engine*
9	BRITISH GP	Brands Hatch	15/07/72	STP March Racing Team	March 721G-Cosworth DFV	
3	Shell Grand Prix	Imola	23/07/72	STP March Racing Team	March 722-Ford BDA	
ret	GERMAN GP	Nürburgring	30/07/72	STP March Racing Team	March 721G-Cosworth DFV	*split oil tank*
dnq	Hitachi Mantorp Grand Prix	Mantorp Park	06/08/72	STP March Racing Team	March 722-Ford BDA	
10	AUSTRIAN GP	Österreichring	13/08/72	STP March Racing Team	March 721G-Cosworth DFV	
3	Levi's Challenge Cup Race	Zandvoort	20/08/72	Alpina Racing Team	BMW 2800CS	*c/d G. Pankl/T. Hezemans*
6	Salzburg Festival Prize	Salzburgring	03/09/72	STP March Racing Team	March 722-Ford BDA	
13	ITALIAN GP	Monza	10/09/72	STP March Racing Team	March 721G-Cosworth DFV	
2	John Player Championship Race	Oulton Park	16/09/72	STP March Racing Team	March 722-Ford BDF	*Fastest lap*
dsq	CANADIAN GP	Mosport Park	24/09/72	STP March Racing Team	March 721G-Cosworth DFV	*outside assistance*
9	Baden-Wurttemberg Prize	Hockenheim	01/10/72	STP March Racing Team	March 722-Ford BDF	
nc	US GP	Watkins Glen	08/10/72	STP March Racing Team	March 721G-Cosworth DFV	
4	Kyalami Nine Hours	Kyalami	04/11/72	Team Gunston	March 73S-BMW	*c/d Jody Scheckter*

1973

ret	ARGENTINE GP	Buenos Aires	28/01/73	Marlboro BRM	BRM P160C	*engine*
8	BRAZILIAN GP	Interlagos	11/02/73	Marlboro BRM	BRM P160C	
ret	SOUTH AFRICAN GP	Kyalami	03/03/73	Marlboro BRM	BRM P160D	*engine*
ret	Race of Champions	Brands Hatch	18/03/73	Marlboro BRM	BRM P160D	*battery lead*
1	Monza Four Hours	Monza	25/03/73	Alpina Racing Team	BMW 3000 CSL	*c/d Brian Muir*
ret	Aspern Saloon Car Race	Aspern	01/04/73	Alpina Racing Team	BMW 2002	*tyres*
5	International Trophy Race	Silverstone	08/04/73	Marlboro BRM	BRM P160D	
ret	SPANISH GP	Montjuich Park	29/04/73	Marlboro BRM	BRM P160E	*tyres*
1	Coupe de Spa	Spa	05/05/73	Alpina Racing Team	BMW 3300 CSL	
7	Spa 1000 KMS	Spa	06/05/73	Alpina Racing Team	BMW 3300 CSL	*c/d Hans Stuck*
5	BELGIAN GP	Zolder	20/05/73	Marlboro BRM	BRM P160E	
dns	Nürburgring 1000 KMS	Nürburgring	27/05/73	Alpina Racing Team	BMW 3300 CSL	*Muir crashed in practice*
ret	MONACO GP	Monte Carlo	03/06/73	Marlboro BRM	BRM P160E	*gearbox*
13	SWEDISH GP	Anderstorp	17/06/73	Marlboro BRM	BRM P160E	
1	Nürburgring 24 Hours	Nürburgring	23/24/06/73	Alpina Racing Team	BMW 3300 CSL	*c/d Hans-Peter Joisten*
9	FRENCH GP	Paul Ricard	01/07/73	Marlboro BRM	BRM P160E	
3	Nürburgring 6 Hours	Nürburgring	08/07/73	Alpina Racing Team	BMW 3500 CSL	*c/d Hans-Peter Joisten*
12	BRITISH GP	Silverstone	14/07/73	Marlboro BRM	BRM P160E	
ret	Diepholz Saloon Car Race	Diepholz	15/07/73	Alpina Racing Team	BMW 3500 CSL	*engine*
ret	DUTCH GP	Zandvoort	29/07/73	Marlboro BRM	BRM P160E	*tyres/fuel pump*
ret	GERMAN GP	Nürburgring	05/08/73	Marlboro BRM	BRM P160E	*accident/wrist injury*
dns	AUSTRIAN GP	Österreichring	19/08/73	Marlboro BRM	BRM P160E	*problems with wrist*
ret	ITALIAN GP	Monza	09/09/73	Marlboro BRM	BRM P160E	*accident*
ret	CANADIAN GP	Mosport Park	23/09/73	Marlboro BRM	BRM P160E	*transmission*
1c	Innsbruck Saloon Car Race	Innsbruck	30/09/73	Alpina Racing Team	BMW 2002	*class win*
ret	US GP	Watkins Glen	07/10/73	Marlboro BRM	BRM P160E	*fuel pump*
1c	End of Season Trophy	Österreichring	14/10/73	Ford Cologne	Ford Capri RS	*class win*

1974

2	ARGENTINE GP	Buenos Aires	13/01/74	Scuderia Ferrari SpA SEFAC	Ferrari 312B3	
ret	BRAZILIAN GP	Interlagos	27/01/74	Scuderia Ferrari SpA SEFAC	Ferrari 312B3	*broken wing*
2	Race of Champions	Brands Hatch	17/03/74	Scuderia Ferrari SpA SEFAC	Ferrari 312B3	
ret	SOUTH AFRICAN GP	Kyalami	30/03/74	Scuderia Ferrari SpA SEFAC	Ferrari 312B3	*ignition/Pole*
ret	Austria Trophäe	Salzburgring	14/04/74	Ford Cologne	Ford Capri RS	*engine/c/d Jochen Mass*
1	SPANISH GP	Járama	28/04/74	Scuderia Ferrari SpA SEFAC	Ferrari 312B3	*Pole/Fastest lap*
2	BELGIAN GP	Nivelles	12/05/74	Scuderia Ferrari SpA SEFAC	Ferrari 312B3	
ret	Nürburgring 1000 KMS	Nürburgring	19/05/74	Ford Cologne	Ford Capri RS	*engine/c/d Jochen Mass*
ret	MONACO GP	Monte Carlo	26/05/74	Scuderia Ferrari SpA SEFAC	Ferrari 312B3	*ignition/Pole*
ret	SWEDISH GP	Anderstorp	09/06/74	Scuderia Ferrari SpA SEFAC	Ferrari 312B3	*transmission*
1	DUTCH GP	Zandvoort	23/06/74	Scuderia Ferrari SpA SEFAC	Ferrari 312B3	*Pole*
2	FRENCH GP	Dijon	07/07/74	Scuderia Ferrari SpA SEFAC	Ferrari 312B3	*Pole*
2	Nürburgring 6 Hours	Nürburgring	14/07/74	Ford Cologne	Ford Capri RS	*c/d T. Hezemans/D. Glemser*
5	BRITISH GP	Brands Hatch	20/07/74	Scuderia Ferrari SpA SEFAC	Ferrari 312B3	*Pole/Fastest lap*
ret	GERMAN GP	Nürburgring	04/08/74	Scuderia Ferrari SpA SEFAC	Ferrari 312B3	*accident/Pole*
ret	AUSTRIAN GP	Österreichring	18/08/74	Scuderia Ferrari SpA SEFAC	Ferrari 312B3	*engine/Pole*
ret	ITALIAN GP	Monza	08/09/74	Scuderia Ferrari SpA SEFAC	Ferrari 312B3	*engine/Pole*
ret	Norisring Saloon Car Race	Norisring	15/09/74	Ford Cologne	Ford Capri RS	*gearbox*
ret	CANADIAN GP	Mosport Park	22/09/74	Scuderia Ferrari SpA SEFAC	Ferrari 312B3	*accident/Fastest lap*
ret	US GP	Watkins Glen	06/10/74	Scuderia Ferrari SpA SEFAC	Ferrari 312B3	*suspension*

1975

6	ARGENTINE GP	Buenos Aires	12/01/75	Scuderia Ferrari SpA SEFAC	Ferrari 312B3	
5	BRAZILIAN GP	Interlagos	26/01/75	Scuderia Ferrari SpA SEFAC	Ferrari 312B3	
5	SOUTH AFRICAN GP	Kyalami	01/03/75	Scuderia Ferrari SpA SEFAC	Ferrari 312T	
1	International Trophy	Silverstone	12/04/75	Scuderia Ferrari SpA SEFAC	Ferrari 312T	
ret	SPANISH GP	Montjuich Park	27/04/75	Scuderia Ferrari SpA SEFAC	Ferrari 312T	*accident/Pole*
1	MONACO GP	Monte Carlo	11/05/75	Scuderia Ferrari SpA SEFAC	Ferrari 312T	*Pole*
1	BELGIAN GP	Zolder	25/05/75	Scuderia Ferrari SpA SEFAC	Ferrari 312T	*Pole*
1	SWEDISH GP	Anderstorp	08/06/75	Scuderia Ferrari SpA SEFAC	Ferrari 312T	*Fastest lap*
2	DUTCH GP	Zandvoort	22/06/75	Scuderia Ferrari SpA SEFAC	Ferrari 312T	*Pole/Fastest lap*
1	FRENCH GP	Paul Ricard	07/07/75	Scuderia Ferrari SpA SEFAC	Ferrari 312T	*Pole*
8	BRITISH GP	Silverstone	19/07/75	Scuderia Ferrari SpA SEFAC	Ferrari 312T	
3	GERMAN GP	Nürburgring	03/08/75	Scuderia Ferrari SpA SEFAC	Ferrari 312T	*pit stop/Pole*
6	AUSTRIAN GP	Österreichring	17/08/75	Scuderia Ferrari SpA SEFAC	Ferrari 312T	*Pole*
3	ITALIAN GP	Monza	07/09/75	Scuderia Ferrari SpA SEFAC	Ferrari 312T	*Pole*
1	US GP	Watkins Glen	05/10/75	Scuderia Ferrari SpA SEFAC	Ferrari 312T	*Pole*

1976

1	BRAZILIAN GP	Interlagos	25/01/76	Scuderia Ferrari SpA SEFAC	Ferrari 312T	
1	SOUTH AFRICAN GP	Kyalami	06/03/76	Scuderia Ferrari SpA SEFAC	Ferrari 312T	*Fastest lap*
ret	Race of Champions	Brands Hatch	14/03/76	Scuderia Ferrari SpA SEFAC	Ferrari 312T2	*brake pipe*
2	US GP WEST	Long Beach	28/03/76	Scuderia Ferrari SpA SEFAC	Ferrari 312T	
2	SPANISH GP	Járama	02/05/76	Scuderia Ferrari SpA SEFAC	Ferrari 312T2	
1	BELGIAN GP	Zolder	15/05/76	Scuderia Ferrari SpA SEFAC	Ferrari 312T2	*Pole/Fastest lap*
1	MONACO GP	Monte Carlo	30/05/76	Scuderia Ferrari SpA SEFAC	Ferrari 312T2	*Pole*
3	SWEDISH GP	Anderstorp	13/06/76	Scuderia Ferrari SpA SEFAC	Ferrari 312T2	
ret	FRENCH GP	Paul Ricard	04/07/76	Scuderia Ferrari SpA SEFAC	Ferrari 312T2	*engine/Fastest lap*
1	BRITISH GP	Brands Hatch	18/07/76	Scuderia Ferrari SpA SEFAC	Ferrari 312T2	*1st place dsq/Pole/Fastest lap*
ret	GERMAN GP	Nürburgring	01/08/76	Scuderia Ferrari SpA SEFAC	Ferrari 312T2	*accident*
4	ITALIAN GP	Monza	12/09/76	Scuderia Ferrari SpA SEFAC	Ferrari 312T2	
8	CANADIAN GP	Mosport Park	03/10/76	Scuderia Ferrari SpA SEFAC	Ferrari 312T2	
3	US GP EAST	Watkins Glen	10/10/76	Scuderia Ferrari SpA SEFAC	Ferrari 312T2	
ret	JAPANESE GP	Mount Fuji	24/10/76	Scuderia Ferrari SpA SEFAC	Ferrari 312T2	*driver withdrew*

1977

ret	ARGENTINE GP	Buenos Aires	09/01/77	Scuderia Ferrari SpA SEFAC	Ferrari 312T2	*fuel metering unit*
3	BRAZILIAN GP	Interlagos	23/01/77	Scuderia Ferrari SpA SEFAC	Ferrari 312T2	
1	SOUTH AFRICAN GP	Kyalami	05/03/77	Scuderia Ferrari SpA SEFAC	Ferrari 312T2	
2	US GP WEST	Long Beach	03/04/77	Scuderia Ferrari SpA SEFAC	Ferrari 312T2	*Pole/Fastest lap*
dns	SPANISH GP	Járama	08/05/77	Scuderia Ferrari SpA SEFAC	Ferrari 312T2	*broken rib in warm up*
2	MONACO GP	Monte Carlo	22/05/77	Scuderia Ferrari SpA SEFAC	Ferrari 312T2	
2	BELGIAN GP	Zolder	05/06/77	Scuderia Ferrari SpA SEFAC	Ferrari 312T2	
ret	SWEDISH GP	Anderstorp	19/06/77	Scuderia Ferrari SpA SEFAC	Ferrari 312T2	*handling*
5	FRENCH GP	Dijon	03/07/77	Scuderia Ferrari SpA SEFAC	Ferrari 312T2	
2	BRITISH GP	Silverstone	16/07/77	Scuderia Ferrari SpA SEFAC	Ferrari 312T2	
1	GERMAN GP	Hockenheim	31/07/77	Scuderia Ferrari SpA SEFAC	Ferrari 312T2	*Fastest lap*
2	AUSTRIAN GP	Österreichring	14/08/77	Scuderia Ferrari SpA SEFAC	Ferrari 312T2	*Pole*
1	DUTCH GP	Zandvoort	28/08/77	Scuderia Ferrari SpA SEFAC	Ferrari 312T2	*Fastest lap*
2	ITALIAN GP	Monza	11/09/77	Scuderia Ferrari SpA SEFAC	Ferrari 312T2	
4	US GP EAST	Watkins Glen	01/10/77	Scuderia Ferrari SpA SEFAC	Ferrari 312T2	

1978

Pos	Race	Circuit	Date	Team	Car	Notes
2	ARGENTINE GP	Buenos Aires	15/01/78	Parmalat Racing Team	Brabham BT45C-Alfa Romeo	
3	BRAZILIAN GP	Rio	29/01/78	Parmalat Racing Team	Brabham BT45C-Alfa Romeo	
ret	SOUTH AFRICAN GP	Kyalami	04/03/78	Parmalat Racing Team	Brabham BT46-Alfa Romeo	*engine/Pole*
ret	US GP WEST	Long Beach	02/04/78	Parmalat Racing Team	Brabham BT46-Alfa Romeo	*ignition*
2	MONACO GP	Monte Carlo	07/05/78	Parmalat Racing Team	Brabham BT46-Alfa Romeo	*Fastest lap*
ret	BELGIAN GP	Zolder	21/05/78	Parmalat Racing Team	Brabham BT46-Alfa Romeo	*accident*
ret	SPANISH GP	Járama	04/06/78	Parmalat Racing Team	Brabham BT46-Alfa Romeo	*engine*
1	SWEDISH GP	Anderstorp	17/06/78	Parmalat Racing Team	Brabham BT46-Alfa Romeo	*fan car/Fastest lap*
ret	FRENCH GP	Paul Ricard	02/07/78	Parmalat Racing Team	Brabham BT46-Alfa Romeo	*engine*
2	BRITISH GP	Brands Hatch	16/07/78	Parmalat Racing Team	Brabham BT46-Alfa Romeo	*Fastest lap*
ret	GERMAN GP	Hockenheim	30/07/78	Parmalat Racing Team	Brabham BT46-Alfa Romeo	*engine*
ret	AUSTRIAN GP	Österreichring	13/08/78	Parmalat Racing Team	Brabham BT46-Alfa Romeo	*accident*
3	DUTCH GP	Zandvoort	27/08/78	Parmalat Racing Team	Brabham BT46-Alfa Romeo	*Fastest lap*
1	ITALIAN GP	Monza	10/09/78	Parmalat Racing Team	Brabham BT46-Alfa Romeo	*1st & 2nd penalised*
ret	US GP EAST	Watkins Glen	01/10/78	Parmalat Racing Team	Brabham BT46-Alfa Romeo	*engine*
ret	CANADIAN GP	Montreal	08/10/78	Parmalat Racing Team	Brabham BT46-Alfa Romeo	*accident*

1979

Pos	Race	Circuit	Date	Team	Car	Notes
ret	ARGENTINE GP	Buenos Aires	21/01/79	Parmalat Racing Team	Brabham BT48-Alfa Romeo	*fuel pressure*
ret	BRAZILIAN GP	Interlagos	04/02/79	Parmalat Racing Team	Brabham BT48-Alfa Romeo	*gear linkage*
6	SOUTH AFRICAN GP	Kyalami	03/03/79	Parmalat Racing Team	Brabham BT48-Alfa Romeo	
ret	US GP WEST	Long Beach	08/04/79	Parmalat Racing Team	Brabham BT48-Alfa Romeo	*accident*
5	Race of Champions	Brands Hatch	15/04/79	Parmalat Racing Team	Brabham BT48-Alfa Romeo	
ret	SPANISH GP	Járama	29/04/79	Parmalat Racing Team	Brabham BT48-Alfa Romeo	*water leak*
ret	Pro-Car Race	Zolder	12/05/79	Marlboro Project Four	BMW M1	*shock absorber*
ret	BELGIAN GP	Zolder	13/05/79	Parmalat Racing Team	Brabham BT48-Alfa Romeo	*engine*
1	Pro-Car Race	Monte Carlo	26/05/79	Marlboro Project Four	BMW M1	
ret	MONACO GP	Monte Carlo	27/05/79	Parmalat Racing Team	Brabham BT48-Alfa Romeo	*accident*
8	Pro-Car Race	Dijon	30/06/79	Marlboro Project Four	BMW M1	
ret	FRENCH GP	Dijon	01/07/79	Parmalat Racing Team	Brabham BT48-Alfa Romeo	*accident*
1	Pro-Car Race	Silverstone	13/07/79	Marlboro Project Four	BMW M1	
ret	BRITISH GP	Silverstone	14/07/79	Parmalat Racing Team	Brabham BT48-Alfa Romeo	*brakes*
1	Pro-Car Race	Hockenheim	28/07/79	Marlboro Project Four	BMW M1	
ret	GERMAN GP	Hockenheim	29/07/79	Parmalat Racing Team	Brabham BT48-Alfa Romeo	*engine*
ret	Pro-Car Race	Österreichring	11/08/79	Marlboro Project Four	BMW M1	*clutch*
ret	AUSTRIAN GP	Österreichring	12/08/79	Parmalat Racing Team	Brabham BT48-Alfa Romeo	*oil leak*
ret	Pro-Car Race	Zandvoort	25/08/79	Marlboro Project Four	BMW M1	*electrics*
ret	DUTCH GP	Zandvoort	26/08/79	Parmalat Racing Team	Brabham BT48-Alfa Romeo	*wrist injury*
2	Pro-Car Race	Monza	08/09/79	Marlboro Project Four	BMW M1	
4	ITALIAN GP	Monza	09/09/79	Parmalat Racing Team	Brabham BT48-Alfa Romeo	
1	Gran Premio Dino Ferrari	Imola	16/09/79	Parmalat Racing Team	Brabham BT48-Alfa Romeo	
dns	CANADIAN GP	Montreal	30/09/79	Parmalat Racing Team	Brabham BT49-Cosworth DFV	*retired after practice*

1982

Pos	Race	Circuit	Date	Team	Car	Notes
4	SOUTH AFRICAN GP	Kyalami	23/01/82	Marlboro McLaren	McLaren MP4-Cosworth DFV	
ret	BRAZILIAN GP	Rio	21/03/82	Marlboro McLaren	McLaren MP4B-Cosworth DFV	*collision*
1	US GP WEST	Long Beach	04/04/82	Marlboro McLaren	McLaren MP4B-Cosworth DFV	*Fastest lap*
dsq	BELGIAN GP	Zolder	09/05/82	Marlboro McLaren	McLaren MP4B-Cosworth DFV	*underweight*
ret	MONACO GP	Monte Carlo	23/05/82	Marlboro McLaren	McLaren MP4B-Cosworth DFV	*engine*
ret	US GP (DETROIT)	Detroit	06/06/82	Marlboro McLaren	McLaren MP4B-Cosworth DFV	*collision*
ret	CANADIAN GP	Montreal	13/06/82	Marlboro McLaren	McLaren MP4B-Cosworth DFV	*clutch*
4	DUTCH GP	Zandvoort	03/07/82	Marlboro McLaren	McLaren MP4B-Cosworth DFV	
1	BRITISH GP	Brands Hatch	18/07/82	Marlboro McLaren	McLaren MP4B-Cosworth DFV	
8	FRENCH GP	Paul Ricard	25/07/82	Marlboro McLaren	McLaren MP4B-Cosworth DFV	
dns	GERMAN GP	Hockenheim	08/08/82	Marlboro McLaren	McLaren MP4B-Cosworth DFV	*injured in practice*
5	AUSTRIAN GP	Österreichring	15/08/82	Marlboro McLaren	McLaren MP4B-Cosworth DFV	
3	SWISS GP	Dijon	29/08/82	Marlboro McLaren	McLaren MP4B-Cosworth DFV	
ret	ITALIAN GP	Monza	12/09/82	Marlboro McLaren	McLaren MP4B-Cosworth DFV	*handling/brakes*
ret	CAESAR'S PALACE GP	Las Vegas	25/09/82	Marlboro McLaren	McLaren MP4B-Cosworth DFV	*engine*

1983

3	BRAZILIAN GP	Rio	13/03/83	Marlboro McLaren	McLaren MP4/1C-Cosworth DFV	
2	US GP WEST	Long Beach	27/03/83	Marlboro McLaren	McLaren MP4/1C-Cosworth DFV	*Fastest lap*
ret	FRENCH GP	Paul Ricard	17/04/83	Marlboro McLaren	McLaren MP4/1C-Cosworth DFV	*wheel bearing*
ret	SAN MARINO GP	Imola	01/05/83	Marlboro McLaren	McLaren MP4/1C-Cosworth DFV	*accident*
dnq	MONACO GP	Monte Carlo	15/05/83	Marlboro McLaren	McLaren MP4/1C-Cosworth DFV	
ret	BELGIAN GP	Spa	22/05/83	Marlboro McLaren	McLaren MP4/1C-Cosworth DFV	*engine*
ret	US GP (DETROIT)	Detroit	05/06/83	Marlboro McLaren	McLaren MP4/1C-Cosworth DFV	*shock absorbers*
ret	CANADIAN GP	Montreal	12/06/83	Marlboro McLaren	McLaren MP4/1C-Cosworth DFV	*spun off*
6	BRITISH GP	Silverstone	16/07/83	Marlboro McLaren	McLaren MP4/1C-Cosworth DFV	
dsq	GERMAN GP	Hockenheim	07/08/83	Marlboro McLaren	McLaren MP4/1C-Cosworth DFV	*reversed into pits*
6	AUSTRIAN GP	Österreichring	14/08/83	Marlboro McLaren	McLaren MP4/1C-Cosworth DFV	
ret	DUTCH GP	Zandvoort	28/08/83	Marlboro McLaren	McLaren MP4/1E-TAG	*brakes*
ret	ITALIAN GP	Monza	11/09/83	Marlboro McLaren	McLaren MP4/1E-TAG	*electrics*
ret	EUROPEAN GP	Brands Hatch	25/09/83	Marlboro McLaren	McLaren MP4/1E-TAG	*engine*
ret	SOUTH AFRICAN GP	Kyalami	15/10/83	Marlboro McLaren	McLaren MP4/1E-TAG	*electrics*

1984

ret	BRAZILIAN GP	Rio	25/03/84	Marlboro McLaren	McLaren MP4/2-TAG	*electrics*
1	SOUTH AFRICAN GP	Kyalami	07/04/84	Marlboro McLaren	McLaren MP4/2-TAG	
ret	BELGIAN GP	Zolder	29/04/84	Marlboro McLaren	McLaren MP4/2-TAG	*water pump*
ret	SAN MARINO GP	Imola	06/05/84	Marlboro McLaren	McLaren MP4/2-TAG	*engine*
2	Inaugural Saloon Car Race	Nürburgring	12/05/84	Daimler Benz AG	Mercedes Benz 190E	
1	FRENCH GP	Dijon	20/05/84	Marlboro McLaren	McLaren MP4/2-TAG	
ret	MONACO GP	Monte Carlo	03/06/84	Marlboro McLaren	McLaren MP4/2-TAG	*spun off*
2	CANADIAN GP	Montreal	17/06/84	Marlboro McLaren	McLaren MP4/2-TAG	
ret	US GP (DETROIT)	Detroit	24/06/84	Marlboro McLaren	McLaren MP4/2-TAG	*electrics*
ret	US GP (DALLAS)	Dallas	08/07/84	Marlboro McLaren	McLaren MP4/2-TAG	*accident/Fastest lap*
1	BRITISH GP	Brands Hatch	22/07/84	Marlboro McLaren	McLaren MP4/2-TAG	*Fastest lap*
2	GERMAN GP	Hockenheim	05/08/84	Marlboro McLaren	McLaren MP4/2-TAG	
1	AUSTRIAN GP	Österreichring	19/08/84	Marlboro McLaren	McLaren MP4/2-TAG	*Fastest lap*
2	DUTCH GP	Zandvoort	26/08/84	Marlboro McLaren	McLaren MP4/2-TAG	
1	ITALIAN GP	Monza	09/09/84	Marlboro McLaren	McLaren MP4/2-TAG	*Fastest lap*
4	EUROPEAN GP	Nürburgring	07/10/84	Marlboro McLaren	McLaren MP4/2-TAG	
2	PORTUGUESE GP	Estoril	21/10/84	Marlboro McLaren	McLaren MP4/2-TAG	*Fastest lap*
ret	Australian Grand Prix	Calder Raceway	18/11/84	Greg Siddle	Ralt RT4-Ford BDA	*accident/Fastest lap*

1985

ret	BRAZILIAN GP	Rio	07/04/85	Marlboro McLaren	McLaren MP4/2B-TAG	*fuel metering unit*
ret	PORTUGUESE GP	Estoril	21/04/85	Marlboro McLaren	McLaren MP4/2B-TAG	*engine*
4	SAN MARINO GP	Imola	05/05/85	Marlboro McLaren	McLaren MP4/2B-TAG	
ret	MONACO GP	Monte Carlo	19/05/85	Marlboro McLaren	McLaren MP4/2B-TAG	*spun off*
ret	CANADIAN GP	Montreal	16/06/85	Marlboro McLaren	McLaren MP4/2B-TAG	*engine*
ret	US GP (DETROIT)	Detroit	23/06/85	Marlboro McLaren	McLaren MP4/2B-TAG	*brakes*
ret	FRENCH GP	Paul Ricard	08/07/85	Marlboro McLaren	McLaren MP4/2B-TAG	*gearbox*
ret	BRITISH GP	Silverstone	21/07/85	Marlboro McLaren	McLaren MP4/2B-TAG	*electrics*
5	GERMAN GP	Nürburgring	04/08/85	Marlboro McLaren	McLaren MP4/2B-TAG	*Fastest lap*
ret	AUSTRIAN GP	Österreichring	18/08/85	Marlboro McLaren	McLaren MP4/2B-TAG	*engine*
1	DUTCH GP	Zandvoort	25/08/85	Marlboro McLaren	McLaren MP4/2B-TAG	
ret	ITALIAN GP	Monza	08/09/85	Marlboro McLaren	McLaren MP4/2B-TAG	*transmission*
dns	BELGIAN GP	Spa	15/09/85	Marlboro McLaren	McLaren MP4/2B-TAG	*wrist injury in practice*
ret	SOUTH AFRICAN GP	Kyalami	19/10/85	Marlboro McLaren	McLaren MP4/2B-TAG	*turbo*
ret	AUSTRALIAN GP	Adelaide	03/11/85	Marlboro McLaren	McLaren MP4/2B-TAG	*accident*

Formula 1 World Championship positions/points

Year	Position	Points	Year	Position	Points
1973	17th=	2	1979	14th	4
1974	4th	38	1982	5th	30
1975	1st	64.5	1983	10th	12
1976	2nd	68	1984	1st	72
1977	1st	72	1985	10th	14
1978	4th	44			420.5

Formula 1 World Championship placings 1st – 6th + Pole + Fastest laps

1st	2nd	3rd	4th	5th	6th	Pole	Fastest lap
25	20	9	7	7	5	24	24